SECRET PETERBOROUGH

June & Vernon Bull

First published 2018

Amberley Publishing
The Hill, Stroud, Gloucestershire, GL5 4EP
www.amberley-books.com

ISBN 978 1 4456 7668 5 (print)
ISBN 978 1 4456 7669 2 (ebook)

British Library Cataloguing in Publication Data.
A catalogue record for this book is available from the British Library.

Origination by Amberley Publishing.
Printed in Great Britain.

Contents

Introduction

So, you think you know Peterborough? This book goes beyond the façade of the familiar to discover the lesser-known aspects of the city's fascinating past. Peterborough has many secrets, like our own Agent Q, and as you wander down its paths you are walking through streets steeped in history. It has been home to visiting kings (Saxon, Norman and medieval) and world-renowned engineers and entrepreneurs, and the city has long been key to Cambridgeshire's industry. There are clear reminders of Peterborough's past everywhere just waiting for you to stop, look and take in their intriguing stories.

Did you know Peterborough was home to the world's first refugees? Or that it boasts a First World War Flying Ace, and shaped Britain's Rembrandt? On a journey through this ancient place, local historians June and Vernon Bull tell these forgotten and lesser-known tales by pulling back the curtains of history to reveal the hidden, strange and the unlikely.

You may think that you know Peterborough, but take another look around and you will find more than you could possibly imagine.

1. Arthur James 'Archie' Robertson, 1908 Olympic Medallist

Arthur was born in 1879, the son of a Glasgow doctor. At the age of fourteen his parents moved to Peterborough where Arthur and his brothers attended King's School, Park Road. He had previously attended Kelvinside Academy in Glasgow. At both schools he was a brilliant all-round sportsman, setting a 1 mile running record at King's School in 1894 that remained unbroken for many years. On leaving school Arthur concentrated on cycling and it was not until he was aged twenty-five that he decided to become a serious athlete.

Representing Peterborough Athletic Club, he finished fifth in the 1906 Amateur Athletic Association Championships and at the end of the season transferred to Birchfield Harriers at Alexandria Stadium, Birmingham.

The following year Arthur took part in four events and gave his best performance in the steeplechase, coming second.

At the age of thirty, after a track and cross-country career lasting four years, Arthur returned to cycling. All his brothers were keen cyclists, especially his youngest brother,

DID YOU KNOW ?

In 1908 Arthur won the English and the International cross-country titles, and by coming second in the 4-mile race that July he earned himself a place in the Olympic team.

Arthur went on to win the 1908 Olympic gold medal in the 3-mile team race, a silver medal in the 3,200-metre steeplechase, and came fifth in the 5-mile race. In the 1908 Olympic season he embarked on a highly successful tour of Scandinavia, and on 13 September in Stockholm he set a world record by running 5,000 metres in 15 minutes and 1.2 seconds.

Peterborough Athletic Club in 1901. Archie Robertson is seated front row in the centre.

Robertson Cycle Merchant seen in the right foreground, Bridge Street.

Dubs Robertson, who also competed in the London 1908 Olympic Games (held at White City) – coming seventh in the finals of the 100-kilometre cycling event.

Arthur owned Robertson's sports and cycle shop at Nos 39–41 Bridge Street and the business was later taken over by his son. Up until 2011 Robertson's cycle shop was still trading from premises in Cowgate until its eighty-two-year-old owner, Mr Peter Upson (not a relative), retired.

Arthur's sports career was certainly varied as he also played football for Peterborough United, later becoming a director of the club. He died at his home in Peterborough on 18 April 1957.

DID YOU KNOW ?

In 2004 Arthur was posthumously inducted into the Scottish Sporting Hall of Fame and in January 2010 a new JD Wetherspoon pub in Perry Bar, Birmingham (close to the former home of the Birchfield Harriers) was named 'The Arthur Robertson' in his honour.

2. Brickyard Passion

There has been a brickmaking tradition in the Peterborough area from as far back as the eighteenth century. These tended to be small yards operating on a seasonal basis and using shallow clays. It wasn't until the 1880s onwards that testing with the lower-lying Oxford clay allowed bricks to be produced on an industrial scale. The latter enabled competition between several companies all aiming to exploit the new process and for many larger companies to buy out the smaller brickmaking yards.

Thus, it is the more unusual partnership between John William Rowe and Matilda Hill (the wife of John Cathles Hill) that becomes intriguing. Apparently, it was Mrs Hill who provided Rowe with a significant portion of the money for him to purchase a plot of

DID YOU KNOW ?

Dogsthorpe brickworks, to the north of Welland Road, was owned by Edward Vergette in the 1860s, Thomas Parker from 1872–90 and then George Cursley from 1890–97. In 1897 the site was sold to John William Rowe who started the Dogsthorpe Brick & Tile Co. Ltd. In 1899 the entire site was put up for auction, but it remained unsold.

land for brickworks at Dogsthorpe level crossing in 1899 (Dogsthorpe Site 2). From 1899 they traded as Star Pressed Brick Co. The company completed several important local orders including the supply of bricks for the new Baker Perkins factories (1904–07), Peter Brotherhood's factory (1906–07) and the factory of Frederick Sage & Co. (1911).

In 1904 Rowe and Mrs Hill bought a 19-acre site at Kings Dyke, Whittlesey where they established another works: the Star Pressed Brick Co. (Whittlesey) Ltd.

Records next show that the Star Pressed Brick Co. (Whittlesey) was incorporated in 1913 and that in 1915 it bought out the Star Pressed (Dogsthorpe) site. Later the Dogsthorpe site

Dogsthorpe brick yard, *c.* 1911.

Star Pressed Brick Co. paperweight.

was owned by the same family who owned the London Brick Co. Ltd and they formally took over the running of the Star Pressed Brick Co. (Whittlesey) in 1923/4.

Rowe appears to have been a very competitive person as he enjoyed shooting, boxing, rowing, hunting and cycling. In fact, he held a world record in cycling in 1889. He was also

DID YOU KNOW ?

John Rowe's interest and involvement in the brick and lime industries came through his business as a local builders merchant. He put great store in the quality of his materials (ornamental bricks, tiles and drainage pipes) and subsequently in 1897 he bought the small brickyard (Dogsthorpe Site 1). Two years later he bought land 0.75 miles further down the road (Dogsthorpe Site 2) with Mrs Hill. He also had an interest in the lime industry and owned kilns at Walton in Peterborough.

a speed skater and came third in the International Amateur Skating Championships at Lingay Fen, Cambridgeshire, in 1890.

The site on Welland Road is today occupied by a variety of two-storey and single-storey dwelling houses, as well as the Calgary Baptist Church on the corner of Welland Road and Poplar Avenue.

3. Buffalo Bill's Wild West Show and the Canadian Mounties

Padholme Road showground was where the old horse racing course used to be, which could be accessed by a dirt track to the north of Padholme Road where Park Lane is today.

Colonel William Frederick Cody, better known as Buffalo Bill, brought his Great Wild West Show to the city on Sunday 14 September 1903. Seven hundred people and 500 horses came to Peterborough East station in three long trains to perform under an amphitheatre at Padholme Road showground on Monday 15 September 1903. For the afternoon performance over 7,000 people attended, and the evening crowd was even bigger.

Buffalo Bill was in his sixties when he came to Peterborough. During the performance he looked like he was floating on air, dressed as a cowboy in an enormous Stetson and astride his pure white stallion 'Beauty', pictured here being unloaded at the East station.

The crowd were treated to cowboys lassoing wild horses and riding bucking broncos. A post pony rider displayed how the mail got through before the coming of the railways and telegraphs.

Buffalo Bill himself gave an impressive exhibition of his skills by shooting from horseback.

DID YOU KNOW ?

Several Native Americans from the Sioux, Arrapahoe, Brime and Cheyenne tribes were in the city on the Sunday evening of the show, and two Indian chiefs even went to the evensong service at St John the Baptist Church.

The Padholme Road showground, although accessed from Padholme Road, also bordered Eastfield Road to the west and Carr Dyke to the east. Several Native Americans from the Sioux, Arrapahoe, Brime and Cheyenne tribes were in the city on the Sunday evening of the show.

Buffalo Bill, 1903.

Buffalo Bill's white horse, Beauty, at Peterborough East station, 1903.

Interestingly, the Eastfield area (west of Eastfield Road) also became home to the Peterborough Agricultural Society showground, which moved from its location in Millfield after 1911. The society purchased 24 acres at a cost of £2,495 in 1909, as it had to vacate the Millfield site earmarked for property redevelopment. A permanent grandstand was built at the Eastfield site in 1936, with seating for 2,000 people at a cost of £7,000. By 1954 the Eastfield showground occupied 46 acres.

In 1965, the agricultural showground moved to its present site at Alwalton. In 1967, the Canadian Mounties came to Alwalton showground, which proved to be a guaranteed crowd puller. From 1969 the site became the home of the East of England showground after a series of mergers that included the Peterborough Agricultural Society.

DID YOU KNOW ?

In 1972 the American Wild West came to Peterborough again (sixty-nine years after Buffalo Bill's visit to the city), but this time the event took place at the East of England showground in Alwalton. This spectacular 'stampede' managed to capture American history with cowboy folklore, Native Americans, outlaws and lawmen. These shows were among the biggest in the country with huge attractions that enthralled the paying public.

4. Charlie Chaplin Comes to Town!

It's a little-known fact that Charlie Chaplin was a frequent visitor to the Empire Theatre in Broadway.

In August 1905 Mr J. Campbell of Grantham purchased the Grand Theatre and it was reopened in December of that year – this time with the name Empire. Some films were shown, but the Empire Theatre mainly offered live music hall performance and

DID YOU KNOW ?

The Empire Theatre began its life as a hall, built by Pye and Hayward for Mr W. Nicholls in 1872. The entrance was on the west. In 1878 a theatre was included in the building, which later became the Theatre Royal with a stage to the west and an entrance onto Broadway. The proprietor between 1890 and 1898 was Mr W. Vernon. The Theatre Royal was again altered to the designs of John Briggs in 1900 and officially reopened on 3 September 1900 as the Grand featuring mainly touring plays.

drama. Eventually, the Empire Theatre closed on 29 November 1959. It lay derelict until early 1961 when it was demolished for the erection of Sheltons department store (now luxury apartments).

Charlie Chaplin was part of Will Murray's touring troop, which came to the city on several occasions. We know that Charlie Chaplin (born in 1889 in London) first came to the city aged seventeen and was a frequent visitor to The Ostrich pub in North Street (a pub built some 180 years ago). It was a popular haunt of stars such as Charlie Chaplin and the rest of Will Murray's touring players, including John Lennon's father Alf (nicknamed Freddie).

Chaplin had a deprived start in life, with his mother succumbing to mental illness and him attending poor schools. Although his parents never divorced they were estranged from around 1891. Charles Chaplin Snr was a music hall entertainer and his mother, Hannah, was a singer when they had Charles Jr. Hannah was committed to a mental asylum and Charles Chaplin Snr became an alcoholic, dying of cirrhosis of the liver.

By the age of thirteen Charlie Chaplin had left school with aspirations of becoming an actor. Using his mother's show business contacts, he became a professional entertainer. His stage credits include *Sherlock Holmes*, followed by a stint with the vaudeville act *Casey's Court Circus*. He appeared at Peterborough's Empire Theatre on Monday 18 January 1906 in Will Murray's *Casey's Court* and took joint billing with Murray. These twice-nightly shows had a cast made up predominantly of children, with Will Murray, as his character Mrs Casey, dressed in drag and failing to keep them in order. Chaplin returned to Peterborough with the Casey Court Players on many occasions between 1906 and 1908.

Chaplin joined the Fred Karno pantomime troupe in 1908, quickly rising to star status as the drunk in *A Night in an English Music Hall*. The Karno act toured America in 1913 and it

Empire Theatre, Peterborough, Monday, Jan. 18.

Above: A flyer for *Casey's Court*, 1906.

Right: An autographed postcard of Charlie Chaplin.

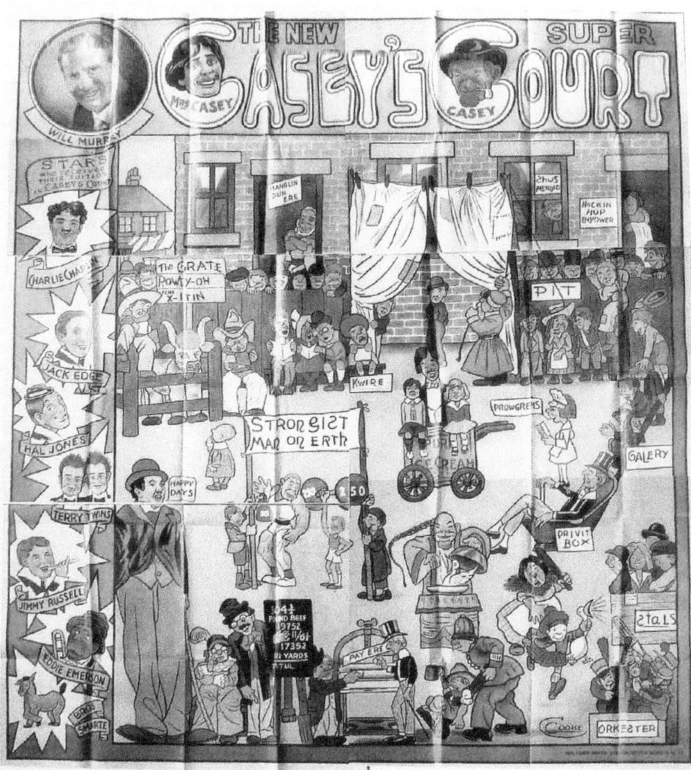

Members of the long-running *Casey's Court* gang show.

was there that Chaplin signed up with Keystone comedy films. In fact, it was while Chaplin was with Mack Sennett (Keystone films) that he came up with his famous 'tramp' screen character who wore an outfit consisting of a too-small coat, too-large trousers, floppy shoes and a battered derby hat. His finishing touch being a postage stamp moustache and a cane used as an all-purpose prop. Thus, Charlie Chaplin's memorable alter screen ego was born!

Chaplin was married four times and had eleven children. He died in Switzerland, aged eighty-eight, in December 1977.

5. Chasing Dreams and Fauna

Dr John Hill was the son of Revd Theophilus Hill and his wife Mary. John was born in Peterborough in 1714 and baptised at St John the Baptist Church on 17 November that year.

Even by eighteenth-century standards John appears to have been a very odd character. At different times he was an apothecary, actor, a theatre critic and, according to the poet Christopher Smart, an 'arch dunce'!

Percy Fitzgerald, a non-contemporary art and theatre critic, said of John:

Above left: Dr John Hill.

Above right: Sir John Hill MD, superintendent of Kew Gardens.

> [He had] scurrilous courage on paper and had no less abject pusillanimity when called to account for his outrages. He had a libellous periodical, called *The Inspector*, which he wrote entirely himself, which earned him in a year no less than fifteen hundred pounds. In this organ he assumes the airs of a public critic and could air his own opinions ... with an amusing vanity.

However, John certainly merits more serious consideration, for he played an important role in the mid-eighteenth century as a theorist on theatre techniques and acting. His book *The Actor* (1750) was a translation of *Le Comédien* by Pierre Rémond de Sainte Albine (first printed in 1747). A second edition of *The Actor* was published in 1755 but this time it was translated back into French as *Garrick ou Les Acteurs Anglais.* The book was well received because of its theories on acting. John argued that as much skill should go into portraying a soldier as a monarch, a bit part as a romantic lead, and maintained that 'playing is a science, and should be studied as a such' and in consequence 'a perfection in the player is the hiding himself in his character'.

A contemporary writes of John that: 'Not only was ... [he] industrious and energetic, but his writings show him to have been a man of real ability and genius.'

During his lifetime John was viewed as conceited, eccentric and keen on self-publicity, and because of this he seems to have had few friends. His quest for wealth and recognition appear to have been marred by these frailties. Although, in retrospect John had many careers: apothecary, practical botanist, actor, gardener (he helped lay out a botanic garden at Kew and was gardener at Kensington Palace) and author (he wrote seventy-six miscellaneous botanical works).

John's huge botanical work *The Vegetable System* (published 1759–75) runs to twenty-six volumes and contains 1,600 engravings of 26,000 different plants. It is considered as one of the most extensive botanical volumes of the eighteenth century.

Though expert and prolific in many subjects, John's life demonstrates the anxieties and paradoxes that existed within Georgian urban life in the 1750s, especially in pleasures and rivalries. Sir John Hill died on 21 November 1775.

DID YOU KNOW ?

Recent research seems to indicate that John was not the quack many portrayed him as. In his 1759 publication he suggests a link between tobacco and cancer.

DID YOU KNOW ?

In 1774 the King of Sweden bestowed upon John the Order of the Vasa (Knight of the Polar Star) in recognition of his services to agriculture. Thus, Dr John Hill became Sir John Hill

6. The Wrong Time

William Joyce, nicknamed Lord Haw-Haw by the *Daily Express*, became a figure of fascination and hate during the Second World War. He began his broadcasts with 'Germany calling, Germany calling'. This was the call sign of a Hamburg radio station that broadcast nightly news bulletins in English to the British people.

Joyce was Irish by blood, American by birth and carried a British passport. He had belonged to Oswald Mosely's British Fascist Party, a political party that attempted to copy Germany's Nazi Party.

Various stories were told by Joyce to unnerve the British public. He told listeners things happening in Britain that he could only have known about through the German spy network established in Britain. One such example was a remark about Peterborough's parish church – St John the Baptist Church –clock on the tower not telling the correct time.

It is widely believed that Lord Haw-Haw warned the enemy by signaling a coded message that our clock was incorrect. This broadcast in 1944 resulted in the death of many French Resistance fighters and that of Captain Thomas Anthony Mellows of the 27th Lancers, Royal Army Corp. Captain Mellows lived at The Vineyard, Cathedral Precincts, with his wife Joyce (née Private, but used the surname Kew). He was the son of William T. Mellows

St John's Church tower with clock.

MBE, LLB, FSA (the moving force behind the publication of the records of Peterborough Abbey and Cathedral) and Beatrice Edith Mellows of Peterborough.

Captain Mellows is buried at Mont de Marsan Cemetery, Landes, south-west France (in Nouvelle-Aquitaine). He is commemorated in the stained-glass window on the north aisle of Peterborough parish church. This window was dedicated in 1968 by the Bishop of Peterborough, Cyril Easthaugh.

DID YOU KNOW ?

Captain Mellows, who was born on 8 March 1920 in Westleigh, Thorpe Road, Peterborough, was captured and killed on 21 August 1944, aged twenty-four, while on special service with the Maquis in the south of France. He was seconded to, and trained with, the Special Operations Executive (working under the codename of Martin during Operation Jedburgh).

At the end of the war, William Joyce was arrested by British Military Police and taken to London where he was tried and found guilty of treason. He was hanged in 1946.

Above left: Captain Mellows in uniform.

Above right: Captain Mellows' grave at Mont-de-Marsan cemetery.

7. Corsets and Parachutes

Between the years 1827 and 1840 three brothers – William, James and Samuel Symington – left Leadshall in Lanarkshire, Scotland, for Market Harborough in Leicestershire. Their uncle was William Symington, who devoted his life to the development of steam engines for ships. He was unsuccessful at exploiting his talents commercially and must have told his nephews many times over about his failure.

William, the eldest of the three brothers, moved away to settle in Market Harborough, a thriving market town. His younger brother James (aged nineteen) soon followed. Within months James set himself up as a tailor, hatter and woollen draper next to the shop where his elder brother William sold tea and coffee. William's shop was thriving and he decided to move into new factory premises to start a food manufacturing company: W. Symington & Co. Ltd. Their third brother Samuel was a commercial traveller and he didn't join his brothers until a few years later.

The former house and shop that William used to own was sold to Mr and Mrs Gold, who had a daughter named Sarah who was skilled at stay making – a craft and trade needed to make corsets. At this time all corsets were handmade and exquisitely embroidered. The combination of Sarah's charm and strong will attracted her neighbour James Symington (who owned the tailor and draper's shop next door) and within three years they were

James and Sarah Symington, *c.* 1847.

married and she had moved into James' drapery business. Their first child was born in 1837 when Queen Victoria came to the throne. Sarah, like the monarch, had nine children but somehow also found time to support her husband's business.

The fashion of the day called for a narrow waist and every woman who could afford to do so (irrespective of her age and figure) wore corsets specially made to constrict her middle to the greatest degree possible. Thus, James was able to advertise himself as a tailor, hatter, haberdasher and stay maker.

In 1850, James and Sarah leased a cottage and set up their very first workroom. All the corsets were hand-made at first, until the advent of the sewing machine – the Singer brand in particular. So, in 1856 James started to take bigger orders, and Market Harborough had one of the first mechanised corset factories in England.

Symington's factory, Peterborough, *c.* 1949.

In the 1860s, corsets became big business in the fashion industry and soon Symington was able to open factories in Leicester, Rugby, Gainsborough, Ipswich, Sudbury, Liverpool, Manchester and Blackwood, as well as Peterborough. James and Sarah Symington's children soon took up positions within the company. Perry Gold Symington, the youngest daughter, joined as an executive as well as a supervisor – unusual in a time when women of her class were expected to stay at home, although working-class girls and young women at this time were known to either enter domestic service or gain factory work. There was keen competition for a job at any of the Symington factories for women who had to work because the conditions were considered far better there.

DID YOU KNOW ?
Symington's Peterborough factory was built in 1903 and housed 250 machines. By 1912 the premises were extended to take a further 200 machines and then ten years later, in 1921, the premises were extended yet again. By the outbreak of the Second World War the Peterborough factory employed 650 people. Between its opening in 1903 and 1956 there were only two factory managers, and a quarter of its workforce had been there for thirty to forty years.

During the Second World War the Peterborough Symington factory made parachutes, tropical shirts and gym shorts, but in the 1950s it reverted to being one of Symington's 'stitching stations'. The Liberty corset or bodice was manufactured at Peterborough.

Sadly in 1967 the business was taken over by Courtaulds and many of the Symington branches and subsidiary companies closed. The Peterborough factory was demolished and is now a residential development. The only legacy is a street called Symington Close (misspelt) in Woodston.

Symington Close today.

8. Earl of Peterborough

The title Earl of Peterborough was created in 1628. The 1st Earl, John, was born in Lowick, Northamptonshire, when Peterborough was part of that county.

Charles Mordaunt, 3rd Earl of Peterborough (1658–1735) was a hero and a friend to the poet Jonathan Swift. The latter viewed Mordaunt as a political ally because of his loyal views on Toryism, and he admired Mordaunt for his bold and difficult character. Mordant seems to have accepted Swift's analysis of him, as letters passed between them with each promising the other to remain 'mighty constant correspondents'.

Alongside Mordaunt's illustrious naval career, he was an active opposition Whig during the last years of Charles II's reign and went to Holland in 1686 to plot with William of Orange. On William's accession to the throne in 1689 Mordaunt was made first Lord of the Treasury and created 1st Earl of Monmouth.

After falling out with the Whigs, Mordaunt demanded the prosecution of Lord John Somers in 1702. Although, bizarrely, in that same year Mordaunt helped Somers with the translations published as *Several Orations of Demosthenes, to Encourage the Athenians to Oppose the Exorbitant Power of Philip of Macedon (1702)*.

In 1705, Mordaunt became joint commander with Sir Cloudsley Shovell of the Spanish expeditionary force. This is when England allied herself with Austria and Holland in opposition to France – with the subject of dispute being the succession to the crown of Spain. That same year Mordaunt (a seasoned military leader and diplomat) led the successful assault on Barcelona, enabling Archduke Charles (later Holy Roman Emperor Charles VI) to be proclaimed King of Spain.

Portrait of the Earl of Peterborough.

The Earl of Peterborough's coat of arms.

Mordaunt was recalled to England in 1707 to explain some of his apparent financial misdeeds and it wasn't until five years later that his career again ascended with special embassies to Frankfurt, Vienna and Italy during the period 1712–13.

His first wife, Carey Fraser, died on 13 May 1709. His future wife, Anastasia Robinson, was only fourteen years of age at this time. It wasn't until Anastasia was aged nineteen that she became a famous singer. She was said to be 'of great beauty and sweetness of disposition'. Born the daughter of Thomas Robinson, a distinguished portrait painter, Anastasia became a friend of the famous composer, George Friedrich Handel.

Being thirty-seven years his junior, society initially didn't accept Anastasia as Mordaunt's wife, instead regarding her as merely his mistress. In fact, her stage work meant that she lived apart from Mordaunt with her two sisters at Parson's Green, London. However, eventually their marriage of some thirteen years was accepted by many. Anastasia, Countess of Peterborough, remained on the operatic stage until 1724 and died in 1755, surviving her husband by twenty years.

DID YOU KNOW ?

In his semi-retirement, and on the accession of George I, Mordaunt secretly married the singer Anastasia Robinson in 1722.

DID YOU KNOW ?

In 1779, Charles Henry Mordaunt (b. 1758) became the 5th Earl of Peterborough. He died aged fifty-five on 16 June 1814 without children, bringing an end to the direct aristocratic line and all titles, including that of Earl of Peterborough. Thus, the then town of Peterborough ceased to have its very own earl.

9. Emily Pankhurst's Visit

Emmeline Pankhurst (14 July 1858 – 14 June 1928) was the founder of the British suffragette movement. She came to talk at Peterborough Corn Exchange, Church Street, on 22 February 1910 about women's emancipation. The movement had been going for six years by this time.

Her influences included Cady, Lucretia Mott and Sarah Remond, who had actively worked for women's rights in America from 1848. Other women who influenced her greatly include Barbara Bodichon, Emily Davies and Elizabeth Garrett, who in 1866 gathered together 1,500 signatures to petition for women to vote in Britain. John Stuart Mill MP moved an amendment to the 1866 Reform Bill to include women on the same terms as men, but this was defeated.

DID YOU KNOW ?

British suffragettes started to employ and develop strategies used in the anti-slavery campaigns: presenting petitions, holding meetings in private homes and public buildings, raising money and using propaganda. They even set up national offices in Westminster to continue to lobby MPs.

In 1903, the suffrage campaign began a new phase, with the Women's Social and Political Union (WSPU) being formed by Emily Pankhurst and her eldest daughter Christabel. Direct action and militancy was advocated using arson, breaking windows, and members tolerating imprisonment and being force-fed. Women across the country soon began to support the WSPU. The latter abandoned its campaign when war broke out in 1914; however, its predecessor, the National Union of Women's Suffrage Society,

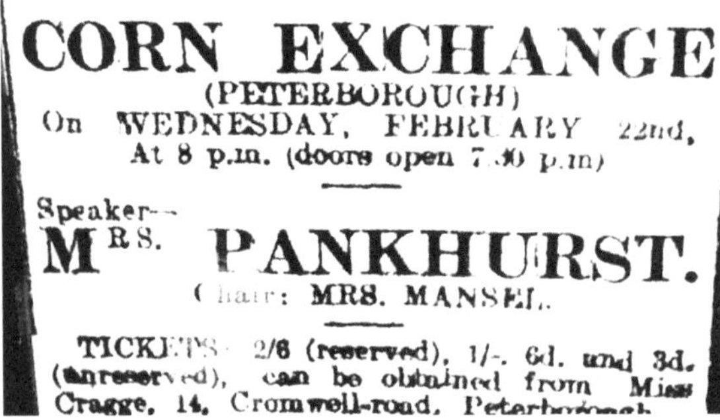

VOTES FOR WOMEN

A PUBLIC MEETING
in the
CORN EXCHANGE
(PETERBOROUGH)
On WEDNESDAY, FEBRUARY 22nd,
At 8 p.m. (doors open 7.30 p.m.)

Speaker—
MRS. PANKHURST.
Chair: MRS. MANSEL.

TICKETS 2/6 (reserved), 1/-, 6d. and 3d. (unreserved), can be obtained from Miss Cragge, 14, Cromwell-road, Peterborough.

Article promoting Mrs Pankhurst's visit to Peterborough.

Above left: 'Votes for Women' postcard.

Above right: Postcard showing a suffragette being forcibly fed.

continued to lobby and in 1918 it managed to secure the vote for women aged over thirty who met minimum property qualifications. The year 2018 marks the centenary of the Representation of the People Act 1918, which allowed some women the right to vote.

Full equal voting still took a further decade of campaigning, however. In 1928, the vote was given to women on the same terms as men, provided they were aged twenty-one or over. Women had finally managed to emancipate themselves.

Emily had exhausted herself physically and mentally with this work, but died aged sixty-nine in the knowledge that that she and her daughters would never be forgotten for their efforts to achieve voting and equal rights for women.

DID YOU KNOW ?

When Emily came to speak at Peterborough Corn Exchange the building was packed with women from across the social spectrum. Some men also attended. Tickets were available from Miss Cragge, a teacher at the County School for Girls, and Mrs Mansel, who was chair of the district WSPU and was in attendance as chair of the Peterborough event.

It is interesting that Christabel Pankhurst spent fifteen years working alongside her mother on women's suffrage. Emily and Richard Pankhurst's second eldest daughter, Sylvia, also campaigned for the suffragette movement as well as anti-fascism. Sylvia left England to settle in Ethiopia with her partner Silvio Corio. She is remembered as a political activist, artist and writer. Her younger sister Adela was given £20 and a ticket to Australia as Emily and Christabel were pushing for the vote for middle-class women, whereas Sylvia and Adela believed in socialism.

10. Noel Keeble, Peterborough's First World War Flying Ace

Noel was born on 6 April 1891 in Thorpe Road and achieved six aerial victories in the First World War. He first flew with 1 Wing Royal Naval Air Service (RNAS) from Dunkirk until the end of 1915. Noel then became flight commander of 202 Squadron and saw quite a lot of action against the German naval units at Flanders.

Noel's achievements include flying for HQ Squadron 1 Wing RNAS in a Nieuport single-seat sport plane. On one occasion, on 25 January 1916, he forced an enemy seaplane to land 7 miles off a French aerodrome.

As a flight sub-lieutenant, he flew for No. 3 Squadron RNSA on 12 November 1916 and was in pursuit of an enemy seaplane, which he had chased from Ghistelles. During this pursuit Noel was flying a Sopworth Pup (N5189), which suffered engine failure and resulted in him having to ditch his plane at sea. Noel was fortunate to be picked up by a French patrol boat *Capricorn* and his seaplane was towed into Calais. Remarkably, the Pup aircraft was salvaged and went on to be used by several other naval squadrons.

Flight Lieutenant Keeble (RNAS) was awarded the Distinguished Service Cross for conscientious gallantry on 23 October 1916 when he attacked four German seaplanes and brought one of them down in a vertical nosedive into the sea, around 10 miles off Ostende.

DID YOU KNOW ?

Noel was subsequently awarded the Distinguished Flying Cross for his exploits on sea patrol when he and an observer obtained 1,000 photographs of enemy positions that were located miles behind enemy lines. He was able to bring home these extremely important new images and information from 5 June 1918 to 16 September 1918, inclusive.

In 1918, Captain Eric Betts was teamed with Captain Keeble in 202 Squadron. Eric Betts went on to become air vice-marshal from 1943 to March 1946 (and was retired in that rank until his death in 1971). It was reported in the *London Gazette* supplement, dated 21 September 1918, that 'Captain Keeble is a most capable and gallant Flight Commander'.

Noel was granted a permanent commission to flight lieutenant in the RAF on 1 August 1919. Two of his three sons followed in his footsteps but tragically were killed while flying combat

Above left: Captain Noel Keeble.

Above right: Flight Lieutenant Keeble.

missions for the RAF during the Second World War. His third son was invalided out of the RAF in 1939 while in training. Noel died in 1963, aged seventy-two, at his home in Chichester.

11. Friendship Across the Waves

There are two Peterboroughs in the USA: one in New Hampshire and the other in New York State (spelt 'Peterboro'). There is also one in Ontario, Canada, and another two are in Australia – one in Victoria and the other in South Australia.

DID YOU KNOW ?

For the first time ever, the six Peterboroughs around the world – including our own – were featured on an international broadcasting link-up on Saturday 19 May 1951. Our city's broadcast came from the City Youth Centre in Bishop's Road and was co-ordinated from a shortwave station called WRUL, Voice of Boston (USA), and lasted half an hour.

The link-up was planned by Professor Carlton Wheeler, a retired modern languages teacher from Peterborough, New Hampshire. Our city's co-ordinator was the late George Dixon who was able to listen to the recording played on a Baird recorder owned by John D'Arcy of D'Arcy the jeweller's in Westgate. The American participants included the head boy of Peterborough High School, New Hampshire; Johanna Sultzmann, a German exchange student there; Mrs Nichols (formerly of Taunton, Somerset), a GI bride who met her husband in the Pacific. Representatives from the two Peterboroughs in Australia included Waye Crowell, a thirteen-year-old high school student and Mrs Meredith Bryant, an Australian war bride from Sydney.

Our city's team, apart from Mr George Dixon, included Mr Lowe, warden of the City Youth Centre, who spoke about the plans for the city's Art Week; Miss Pat Barrows, who talked about hockey and swimming and sailing facilities in the city; Miss Margaret Amps, a member of the Clarion Cycling Club; Mr Christopher Eyres, city planning assistant, member of the Mask Theatre and cricket enthusiast; Mr Alex Taylor, secretary of the Peterborough and District Youth Sports Association; and Mr John D'Arcy, chairman of the Youth Executive Council.

During the broadcast, Professor Wheeler explained that it was his hope that this link-up would be the first of many and that relationships could be enhanced further by an interchange of news and views between the Peterboroughs and their citizens of similar trades and professions.

Some interesting facts about the six Peterboroughs are that the Peterborough in Canada used to be known as the 'electric city', as it was one of the first in Canada to use electric streetlights. Peterborough, New Hampshire, is home to the first free public library (founded on 9 April 1833) in the United States. Peterboro, New York State, USA, is home to the National Abolition Hall of Fame and Museum, which honours anti-slavery abolitionists and their work to end slavery along with the legacy of that struggle, which today focuses on the moral conviction to end racism. Peterborough, Victoria, Australia, is a fishing town and Peterborough in South Australia is known for its agriculture – mainly wheat. Peterborough, England, remains one of the fastest growing cities in the UK. It has a history of successful economic growth and acts as an attractor for investment.

Peterborough, New Hampshire, *c.* 1908.

Peterborough, Ontario, 1977.

Some notable people associated with the six Peterboroughs include Ontario architect Eberhard Zeidler who designed the Eaton Centre in Toronto. Peterborough, New Hampshire, USA, produced its fair share of congressmen with the Bass' and Wilsons. Peterborough, Victoria, Australia, is home to amateur radio enthusiast John Young (who used to live in St Ives, Cambridgeshire). Peterborough, South Australia, was home to newspaper proprietor William H. Bennett. Peterborough, New York State, was the birthplace of Greene Smith, renowned ornithologist. Peterborough, England is associated with many famous people, among the many is the eminent aerospace engineer and Peterborian Arthur Rowledge MBE, FRS (1876–1957).

12. Henshaw Barrel Rolls the Big Bomber

Alexander Adolphus Dumfries Henshaw was born in Peterborough on 7 November 1912 and was a 1930s record-breaking racing pilot, author and businessman.

The eldest son of a wealthy farmer, Alex, as he liked to be known, gained a passion for flying from the age of nineteen in Skegness when he joined the East Lincolnshire Aero Club. He made a name for himself in the King's Cup Races flying against such legendary pilots as Captain Sir Geoffrey de Havilland (his cousins being the Hollywood film stars and stage actresses Olivia de Havilland and Joan Fontaine).

DID YOU KNOW ?

Henshaw's father bought him a De Havilland Gipsy Moth in 1931 and within a year he gained his private pilot licence – on 6 June 1932. Six years later Alex was winning trophies for his flying. In 1938, he won a solo record to Cape Town, departing in his Aerial Mew Gull plane from Gravesend in the record time of 39 hours and 23 minutes.

Henshaw, 'King of Speed'.

With the outbreak of the Second World War he sought a job at fighter command, saying: 'I want to join a unit by the name of Special Duty Flight, which basically means I get into a reconnaissance plane – take a photo of a target, come back, get into another more suitable plane and bomb the hell out of it.'

Many people only remember Alex as a test pilot of Spitfires but he flew many other aircraft, including the Hurricane, Wellington and Lancaster. In fact, he became the only man known to victory roll a Lancaster bomber; ground crew and fellow pilots verified this task of sheer brilliance.

He is best remembered as one of the many great Spitfire test pilots at Castle Bromwich from 1940–1946, and personally flew over 3,000 flights. The job was not without its dangers as several test pilots were killed and some 130 forced landings were made – of which Alex had his fair share, surviving a significant engine failure with confidence.

As a test pilot he kept a strict routine and the longest day he worked was from 3.15 a.m. to midnight the same day! Every time Alex took a plane into the air the thought of a crash landing was always at the forefront of his mind. No matter where he was, crash landing sites were mapped, and approaches lined up. The thought of giving up flying without finding the cause of the failure was failure itself, as far as he was concerned.

DID YOU KNOW ?

For his services during the war Henshaw was appointed MBE, but many thought this insufficient reward for his great contribution to flying. In fact, defence chiefs stopped him from fighting in the war because he was considered too valuable and the founder of the Battle of Britain Society, Bill Bond, acknowledged Alex Henshaw as the greatest pilot Britain had seen.

Alex on a test flight in his Mew Gull.

After the war Alex was emotionally and physically drained so he left England to start a career in the aircraft industry for Miles Ltd of South Africa. Two years later he returned to take over the family farming and holiday business in Skegness.

Aged ninety-four, Alex, who survived his wife Barbara (widow of Count de Chateaubrun who also flew Mew Gull aircraft) by eleven years, died at his home in Newmarket on 24 February 2007 and is survived by his only son Alexander Jr.

It is thought that Henshaw Park in Parnwell is named after Alex. The park was officially opened in February 2012 by the Worshipful Mayor of Peterborough, Councillor Paula Thacker MBE.

13. The Civilian Repair Depot, Horsey Toll

Search lights and anti-aircraft guns located at Horsey Toll (just outside Stanground) gave a clue as to what was nearby during the Second World War. The primary duty of both was to protect the Civilian Repair Depot (CRD) located at a former private landing field at Shortacres Farm (2.5 miles east of Peterborough), belonging to Mr Hugh Abinger Whittome and later his son Kenneth Whittome. The airfield was licenced in May 1930.

The Horsey Toll airfield was closed on the outbreak of the Second World War, later becoming a CRD that repaired aircraft – Hurricanes and parts of Wellingtons. RAF Westwood was also close by.

It was in 1940 that Lord Beaverbrook, the Minister of Aircraft Production, established an organisation in which a number of manufacturers were seconded to repair and overhaul battle-damaged Hurricanes. The Civilian Repair Organisation (CRO) also overhauled other battle-weary aircraft, which were later sent to training units or to other air forces. One of the companies involved was Morrisons Engineering Ltd, Purley Way, Croydon (Croydon 0191-2). They were aeronautical and general engineers who specialised in aircraft assemblies, sub-assemblies, covered components, tool making, press work, air/ground systems parts, welding, sheet metal work and all kinds of machining, heat treatment, anodising and cadmium plants.

DID YOU KNOW ?

During the Second World War, Morrisons Engineering Co. Ltd purchased Horsey Toll airfield and converted the aircraft hangars into factory units where cotton fabric was used on aircraft wings and then doped. Aircraft dope is a plasticised lacquer that is applied to fabric-covered aircraft. It tightens and stiffens fabric stretched over airframes, which renders them airtight and weatherproof.

Typical doping agents include nitrocellulose, cellulose acetate and cellulose acetate butyrate. Liquid dopes are highly flammable – nitrocellulose, for instance, is also known as the explosive propellant 'guncotton'. Dopes often include colouring pigments to facilitate even application and are available in a wide range of colours.

One such worker at Horsey Toll was Mrs Kathleen Church who is pictured here with her treasured wing badge and part of a Hurricane wing made into a wooden key. She worked with six other women within one section of the Civilian Repair Unit. She recalls Mr Wainman as the manager and the foreman being Mr Stonebridge.

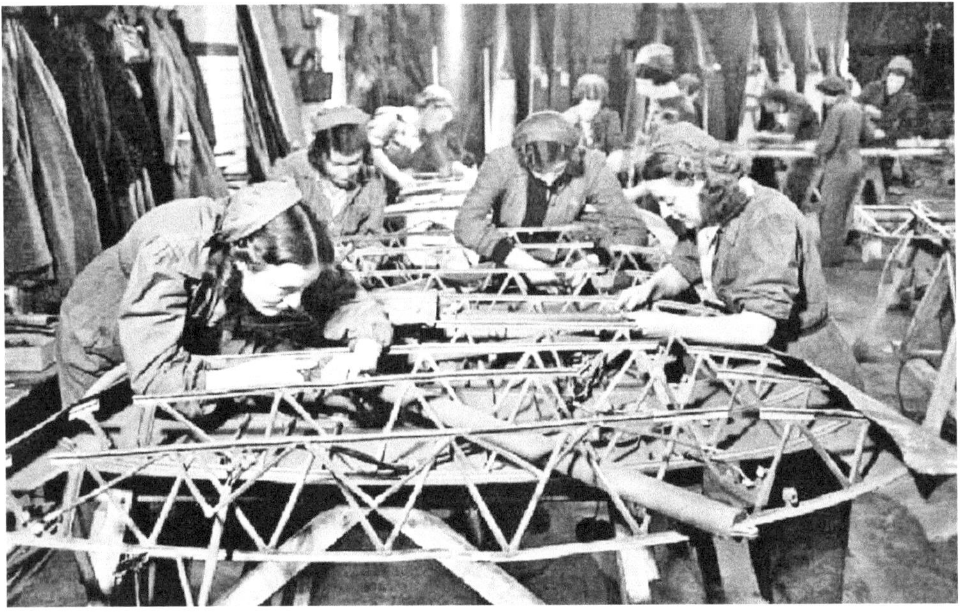

Civilian workers carrying out salvage and repair work on a wing.

DID YOU KNOW ?

Horsey Toll CRD would repair aircraft engines, air frames, broken fuselages, tail planes and ailerons.

The CRD fixed the most damaged aircraft. In mid-July 1940, it was returning 160 a week to service and it had put back into service a total of some 4,955 aircraft by December 1940. Thus, a little-known local factory helped the war effort in a way that is much forgotten today.

Right: Mrs Kathleen Church with her memorabilia.

Below: Horsey Toll today.

14. Hounds of Fletton Tower

Fletton Tower, a Victorian stately home accessed from Queens Walk, was built in the Gothic style between 1841 and 1847 for William Lawrence – a local solicitor, coroner, and Justice of the Peace for the Soke of Peterborough. Fletton Tower used to sit in quite a large area of land, taking in parts of what is now Orchard Street (once part of the orchard at Fletton Tower), Queens Walk and Bread Street, and the property could also be accessed from an archway on Oundle Road. It is fair to say the estate straddled the border of New Fletton and Woodston.

After William Lawrence the property's next owner (in the 1860s) was Thomas Mills, who made his money in Bradford as a cabinet, carpet and feather warehouse proprietor. Mills sold the property in 1881. Eventually, Harry Bark Hartley (father of the celebrated novelist L. P. Hartley and respected Scottish deerhound breeder Norah Hartley) bought the property in 1900. Harry Hartley was a well-known Peterborough solicitor, public speaker and local Liberal councillor for West Ward. The house was built following the principle that as many rooms should face the south as possible. It has an embattlement tower rising above the entrance. The windows have stone mullions and transoms. Over the front doorway is an oreil window carved with the initials of Thomas Mills, who bought the house in the 1860s and added a new kitchen and boot room among others.

The lofty central entrance hall contains a timber staircase in the Gothic style, and the ceiling above has paintings dated 1864 with the initials of Thomas Mills. The dining room to

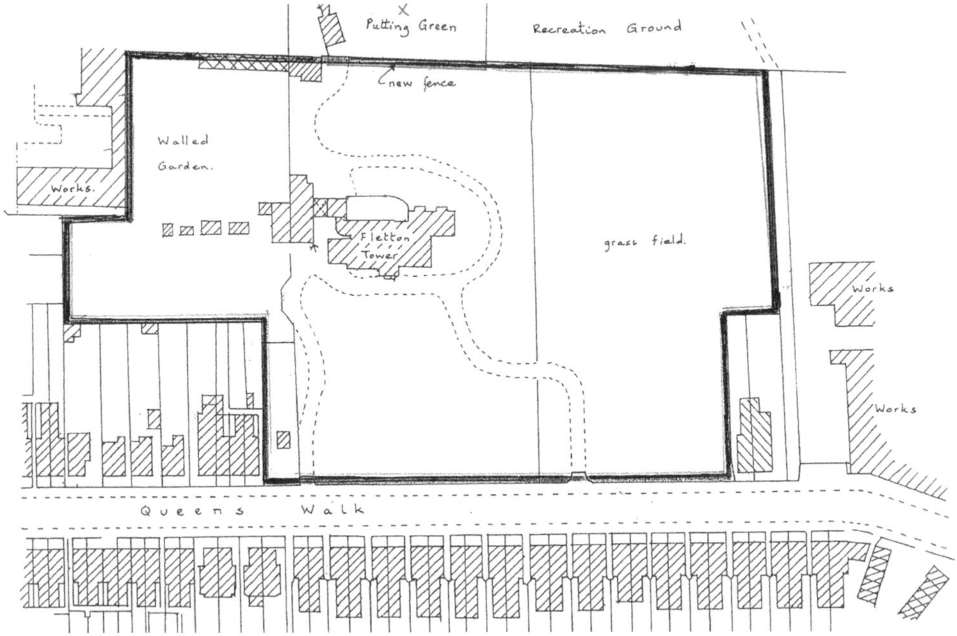

Extent of the estate in 2010.

the east has a fireplace with an Early English Gothic surround under one of the windows. The drawing room to the north wing has a richly foliated iron fire grate above a hearth covered with radiating iron bars, all within an eighteenth-century French-style marble fireplace. Doors to the principal rooms have panels carved with linen fold and other Tudor-style decoration. Outbuildings and a conservatory to the north-west continue the style of the house.

DID YOU KNOW ?

Up until its demolition in 1974 a stone gateway to an avenue which is entered from Oundle Road via a gate tower formed an entrance to Fletton Tower.

The Hartley family occupied the property for nearly a century. At an early age Leslie Poles Hartley was encouraged to write by his aunt who lived in London, romance novelist Kathleen Lund. In later life Leslie said that the book that stood out as his easiest to write was *Simonetta Perkins* (1925), which he completed within a fortnight. His favourite story, *The Go-Between* (1953) was one of his most popular and was written when he lived in Venice. It was adapted by Harold Pinter and made into a film in 1970. The book's opening line, 'The past is a foreign country: they do things differently there', has become well known and is often quoted.

L. P. Hartley's sister, Norah, was the youngest of Harry and Bessie Hartley's children and she was totally wrapped up in breeding and showing Scottish deerhounds. The dogs had the run of Fletton Tower when Norah was the only surviving resident. We had the great

Oundle Road gatehouse before demolition.

pleasure of meeting her in the late 1980s and found her totally engaging and quite charming. Her best dogs were Fly and Fall. Norah would often be asked to judge at Montrose, Scotland. Her absolute joy was winning the hound group at Crufts with Betsinda in 1982. Her other treasured memory was becoming the first female board member of the Kennel Club.

DID YOU KNOW ?

It was on the death of Norah Hartley (celebrated Scottish deerhound breeder) in 1994 that the Hartley family occupancy of Fletton Tower came to an end. In 1995 the contents of the tower came under the hammer at Sotheby's and a staggering £300,000 was raised at the auction. Two Venetian oil paintings (*The Doge's Palace in Venice* and *The Grand Canal*) were snapped up for £46,600. An oak table, dating back to around 1710, and a Turkish silk rug sold for just under £6,000 each. Out of the 421 lots, ten were bought by the descendants of the Hartleys and thirty-three went unsold.

In 1996, Fletton Tower was sold for around £350,000 to Terry Marriott. Presently Fletton Tower is occupied by Christopher Poulter and his wife Joanne (a celebrated Chelsea Flower Show exhibitor and demonstrator who owns Bespoke Buds, Peterborough).

In 2010, they added a new cloakroom in place of the laundry room, the boot room became a family room and the utility room became a new hall. Fletton Tower remains in private hands and is not open to the public. It was given Grade II-listed status on 26 February 1980.

Fletton Tower today.

15. The Huguenots

No. 11 Bridge Street was a rather splendid and historic house, locally referred to as the Huguenot House. The front was designed in the Inigo Jones style and was built in around 1748. The first occupant of this house was Monsieur James Delarue, a French refugee and merchant banker. He was also a Huguenot.

As refugees, Protestant exiles from France in the reign of Louis XIV (who built Versailles and was known as the Sun King), the Huguenots fully integrated into British society and made their presence felt in banking, commerce, industry, the book trade, the arts, the military, on the stage and in teaching. Some 40,000–50,000 came to England during the late 1660s and early 1700s, with more arriving during periods of persecution in France in the mid-eighteenth century.

DID YOU KNOW ?

The Huguenots were first and foremost Protestants and they were distinctive in their social divisions. Most men and women in France – as in England – were directly employed in agriculture, yet few Huguenots that came to England were workers of the land. The majority lived in towns. They were artisans (especially weavers) and those that came to Britain and Ireland included skilled craftsmen, silversmiths, watchmakers and professional people – clergy, doctors, merchant soldiers and teachers – with a small sprinkling of the lesser nobility.

Huguenot House, No. 11 Bridge Street.

DID YOU KNOW ?

When the Delarues occupied No. 11 Bridge Street it had a sumptuous staircase with the walls covered in leather panels, all hand-painted with exquisite Oriental scenes.

Above: Murals on the stair walls.

Left: Library.

They maintained their Protestant (Calvanist) religion while in Peterborough and many attended our parish church. There are two monuments to the left of the west door of this church (St John the Baptist Church) that remain as testament to the fact that our city, and indeed our church, made the Huguenots most welcome. James Delarue's remains lie in a vault behind a monument commemorating the death of his wife Sarah and his sister (also named Sarah) who each pre-deceased him. James died on 12 March 1782 at his home No. 11 Bridge Street. Adjacent to this monument is one that commemorates the death of James' sister Ann Pulvertoft, who died 12 April 1788 aged eighty-one.

Later, No. 11 Bridge Street (roughly the site of today's Sue Ryder charity shop) was occupied by the Colemans (of the company Cadge & Coleman Ltd who were later bought out by Whitworths flour) from October 1856 to September 1920. In 1927, the premises was occupied by the Post Office (with this branch run by Miss Searle) and later it was the offices of the National Fuel Oil Co. Ltd.

16. Last Man to be Publically Hanged

David Thompson Myers, a married man with six children who worked as a linen draper in Stamford, was the last person to be executed in Peterborough. He was hung in public on Monday 11 May 1812 outside Fengate Gaol, located at the corner of Padholme Road and Carr Dyke. This was his punishment for confessing to an act of homosexuality.

Myers was held in the Abbot's Gaol (Kings Lodgings, formerly Reba, on Cathedral Square) and according to accounts in the *Stamford Mercury* he was hung in front of a crowd of 5,000. The population of the city at this time was 3,500, indicating many had travelled to the city for this day of entertainment. Executions were public spectacles and the atmosphere could sometimes be quite festive, although riots occasionally broke out.

DID YOU KNOW ?

At public executions there was often sympathy for the person about to be hanged and the crowd would jeer the hangman. The reputed dying speeches of the condemned person (sometimes written for them) were printed and sold at great profit to the gathered crowd.

Myers' crime was sodomy. This was during a period where over 200 crimes carried the death penalty, including stealing and burglary. His crime was heard in the assize court (now crown court) and he was found guilty of a homosexual act in Burghley Park; the other chap got away.

He took the holy sacrament on Friday from Revd Joseph Stephen Pratt LLB, vicar of St John the Baptist Church and prebendary to the cathedral. Myers' coffin was placed with him in his cell, at his wish, and at 11.15 on Monday 11 May 1812 he took his seat in a chaise accompanied by a clergyman. The hearse containing the coffin to receive his body went ahead of him in his full sight. In around thirty minutes he reached the tree where a new drop had been erected. He knelt in prayer and the vicar used the prayers they had composed during his term of imprisonment. Myers concluded with the Lord's Prayer and said a few words to the people, confessing his crime and exhorting them.

When the executioner was putting the rope round his neck he assisted in opening the collar of his shirt. The nightcap was placed on his head and he then threw down the skin of

DID YOU KNOW ?

As the nineteenth century progressed it was realised that such public spectacles did not deter criminals but encouraged troublemakers and allowed thieves easy pickings from the onlookers. As such, the Prisons Act of 1868 made it mandatory that all future executions were to take place within the prison walls.

an orange he had been sucking and pulled the cap over his face. The executioner then left to undo the bolts that supported the drop, and in minutes Myers was dead.

Several days before his execution Myers made his confession, which was signed on 2 May 1812 in the presence of the vicar of Peterborough, the Clerk of the Peace and a Peterborough attorney.

Details of the execution made front page news in *The English Chronicle* and *Whitehall Evening Post* on Tuesday 12 May 1812.

D. T. MYERS,

TWO DAYS PREVIOUS TO HIS

EXECUTION,

And left by him with a request that the same might be made public after his Death.

AS I believe that Persons in my unhappy Situation are expected to say something at the Place of Execution, and feeling that I shall not be able to do it, I wish these my Dying Words to be inserted in the Stamford *Papers*, and to be made as public as possible. I confess that I am guilty of the Crime for which I am about to suffer; and for these and all my Sins, I desire to repent before God with a broken and contrite Heart. I forgive from the bottom of my Soul, every one who has wronged me, and I earnestly pray to Almighty God that *my untimely end may be a warning to others, who are walking in the same path.* Oh! may my shameful Death put a stop to that dreadful Crime! *may those who have been Partakers with me in my Crimes be brought to true Repentance! !* I am a miserable Sinner in the sight of God, and I am deservedly degraded in the sight of Man. But I commit my guilty polluted Soul into the hands of my Blessed Saviour, to be pardoned and cleansed by him. And tho' I deserve nothing but Punishment for my Sins, I trust, thro' the merits of my Redeemer, when I leave this wicked and miserable World, to be received into a World of Purity and Peace.

As my Example has led many into Sin, I hope these, my Dying Words, may *lead many to Repentance.*

D. T. Myers.

Signed in Peterborough Gaol, 2d of May, 1812.

IN THE PRESENCE OF

J. S. PRATT, Vicar of Peterborough.
JOHN ATKINSON, Clerk of the Peace.
THOs. ATKINSON, Attorney, Peterborough.

Myers' death confession.

17. Latvian Valters, Peterborough's Strongman

Peterborough strongman and daredevil Walter Cornelius was born Valters Cornelius in Latvia in 1923. He spent his adulthood as a swimming pool attendant. His most notable achievements were: winning the world sausage-eating championship in 1966 after finishing off twenty-three bangers in ten minutes; attempting to defy gravity by flying across the River Nene dressed as a birdman; pushing a double-decker bus for half a mile using his head; eating 3lbs 8ozs of raw onions in two minutes and two seconds; and pushing a pea with his nose up Castor Hill with his agent and friend Helga Jansons. There was nobody bigger or better than Peterborough's strongman.

Walter was an incredibly brave teenager who in the 1940s made it through the Iron Curtain to Peterborough after rowing 400 miles across the Baltic Sea from Latvia to Sweden while the Russians took pot-shots at him. The giant bullet holes that remained in his stomach and back were testament to his amazing courage and strength. This kind, gentle giant of a man made his home in Peterborough in a caravan and dedicated his life to making others cheery and raising a fortune for charity. Other Latvians in the city to whom he was a friend included the above Helga and Mr and Mrs Ozols of Lime Tree Avenue (whose daughter Laima was a school friend of Helga's).

DID YOU KNOW ?

Walter apparently ate onions like they were pears and liked to walk on his hands up the Lido steps (being a lifeguard there for a number of years) with a tray of tea balanced on his feet, before bending old pennies with his teeth to amuse the kids.

Helga and Walter pea pushing.

Walter carrying children.

His remarkable charity feats saw him appear on *Opportunity Knocks* and *Blue Peter,* but it was never about the fame for him. Concrete blocks were smashed over his head, motorbikes rode over his chest, he rolled peas and cannonballs with his nose and he carried children – eight at a time – in a swing balanced on his head.

Walter's most famous stunt involved trying to fly off the top of Brierley's supermarket on Bridge Street and across the Nene. He knew he would fail but he went ahead anyway. His reward was £300, a year's groceries and a broken nose!

DID YOU KNOW ?

Peterborough's adopted hero Walter Cornelius is now remembered with a weather vane hanging above the Lido swimming pool and a bistro named after him at the Broadway Theatre.

Sadly, having brought so much joy and laughter into the lives of many, Walter died all alone at the age of sixty on 23 September 1983. He was found dead in the car he was sleeping in. Walter was buried in Eastfield cemetery, and some ten years after his death those that remembered him with fondness raised enough money to have a headstone placed on his grave. To this day many remember Walter with great affection and recount the fact that in 1964 he was the world's strongest man.

18. Peterscourt and Sir George Gilbert Scott

Peterscourt, located in City Road, was designed by architect Sir George Gilbert Scott, famous for planning St Pancras station, the Prince Albert Memorial and the Foreign Office. He was master of the Gothic Revival and designed 800 buildings in England alone. He produced churches, schools, colleges, hospitals, workhouses, asylums and vicarages aplenty. Sir George Scott has 607 structures listed as historic – more than any other architect (next is Sir Edwin Lutyens with 402).

Peterscourt was built between 1856 and 1859 and was opened in 1864 as St Peter's College, a Church of England teacher training college for men. It is constructed of red brick and has paired lancet-headed windows with head diapered brick in recess along with patterns in a blue-black brick. Its main doorway was brought from the London Guildhall, which was damaged in the Blitz in 1940. The Guildhall door is made of early eighteenth-century wood and has finely carved Corinthian pilasters with swags on a frieze and a rectangular fanlight with Gothic-style glazing.

The college boasted a large hall, dining hall, art room, library, common rooms, a well-fitted science laboratory and nature study rooms. In addition, there was a hostel within the cathedral precincts within a three-minute walk of the college. The hostel had extensive grounds and provided accommodation for forty-four resident students, with fifty-one resident students being housed in the college itself.

Sir George Gilbert Scott RA.

St Peter's common room, 1910.

External view in 1949.

DID YOU KNOW ?

At the onset of the First World War the building closed as a training college for men and it wasn't until October 1921 that it reopened – as a women's teacher training college. In 1938, it closed again and during the Second World War it was used as an American Service Club and as the centre for the American Red Cross. After the war, in 1946, it reopened as an emergency training college for men and in 1949 it became a mixed college, only to close a year later

In 1952, the college was bought by Frank Perkins Engines Ltd who internally refurbished the building to turn it into offices. They also reroofed it and changed its named from St Peter's to Peterscourt. Perkins ceased to occupy the building in 1967. In the following year until 1975 the Peterborough Development Corporation had its offices there. It was during the PDC's occupancy that the building was listed as a Grade II structure on 7 May 1973.

From 1984 to 1986 the building underwent a refurbishment and restoration phase with the additions that were made to the building in the 1950s being removed and the main entrance was relocated from the northern side to the western end. Also, a new Gothic porch was built to contain the doorway from the Guildhall in London. The whole of the internal space was fully refurbished and today the building is used as offices for organisations like Opportunity Peterborough, Eco-Innovation Centre, Architectural Design Consultancy, Archway Construction (UK) Ltd, and many others.

19. A Local Star

Harold and Iris Thompson lived at Colebrook, Cherry Orton Road, Orton Waterville (the opposite side of the road close to the Windmill Pub) and were the proud parents of a daughter who went on to become the versatile and effective cameo actress Fanny Carby.

Fanny was born in Sutton Coldfield on 2 February 1925. She made a living playing character parts and despite the lion's share of her work being cameo appearances, she did take on weightier roles including portraying Vera Duckworth's domineering mother Amy Burton in twenty-three episodes of *Coronation Street* in 1987 and 1988.

Fanny was one of the founder members of Joan Littlewood's Theatre Workshop in Stratford East, occupying the derelict Theatre Royal from 1953. Today the theatre still has a community focus and promotes new and multicultural work. Joan Littlewood's Theatre was created by a group of actors committed to a left-wing ideology. The idea had germinated after the Second World War and looked to settle in Glasgow but ended up in East London.

Fanny Carby was a friend of Peter Pollock who was closely associated with Stalin's Hertfordshire spy Guy Burgess. The latter loved to sit round the fire at Sharlowes Farm in Flaunden, Hertfordshire (owned by Peter Pollock, part-heir to Accles and Pollock, a light engineering company in Birmingham). The farm was an open house to painters like Francis Bacon, writers, actors and actresses, including Fanny who described Guy Burgess as 'terribly likeable'. Fanny said Guy loved coming down to the farm as he liked to be cosy. He liked people making cups of tea and pie crusts and he had a charisma, a sort of fatal fascination. It wasn't just charm. You were always so glad to see Guy.

Burgess continued to visit Peter Pollock at Flaunden until he defected to Russia with fellow traitor Donald Maclean in May 1951.

Although best remembered for screen work, Fanny's happiest days were spent at Joan Littlewood's Theatre Workshop. The highlight of her years was her role as one of the Pierrots in *Oh, What a Lovely War*, expertly produced in 1963 by Joan Littlewood. The play viewed the First World War from the perspective of the common soldier and it counterpointed various melodies from the period with the grim battle statistics that appeared in a running newsreel tape above the stage. The play went on to be performed

Fanny Carby, *c.* 1960.

DID YOU KNOW ?

Fanny Carby would return to Orton Waterville on numerous occasions to visit her parents and take part in various village fêtes and charity events. Her film roles included parts in *The Elephant Man* (1980) and *Mrs Galloway* (1997) and she played TV parts in *Dixon of Dock Green, Z Cars, On The Buses, Maigret, Heartbeat, Goodnight Sweetheart, Birds of a Feather* and *Middlemarch* to name but a few.

on Broadway, and Fanny was one of its critically acclaimed cast members. Fanny died in London aged seventy-seven on 20 September 2002.

20. Mac Sneath, a Local Unsung Hero

John Macilwain Sneath, known as 'Mac', was born on 1 February 1909 at No. 236 Lincoln Road, Millfield, Peterborough, in the house that his father John James 'Jack' Sneath had

DID YOU KNOW ?

Mac attended Deacon's School, where pupils were called 'donkeys' by boys attending King's School. This was all part of the good-natured rivalry that existed between the two grammar schools.

inherited from his father. The family had come from three generations of stonemasons before Mac's father changed the business to a builders' merchant using the same premises.

One of Mac's teachers reported that he wished Mac showed the same interest in schoolwork as he did in building crystal sets! Mac would often play truant – to the despair of his father – but despite this lack of interest in education, in later life he was keen to attend school reunions. Despite his poor attendance he went on to achieve more than his fellow scholars.

Mac trained as a draughtsman before inheriting the family firm, builders' merchants John Sneath Ltd at Nos 232/236 Lincoln Road. His future wife, Alice Tooke, known as 'Mary', worked next door in the accounts department of H. Crussells Ltd (wholesale electrical goods, ironmongers, builders' merchants, and general-purpose store) at No. 238 Lincoln Road. Both were members of the Peterborough Ramblers' Club. The couple eventually married on 27 August 1943 at St Mary's Church, New Road.

Mac, like his father, attended St Barnabas Church, Gladstone Street, and was the churchwarden and a keen campanologist during the 1950s.

After training in 1942, he served in the Navy under the Admiralty Yachtsman Emergency Services Scheme in 1944. Mac volunteered on an auxiliary war vessel, MFV (motor fishing vessel), employed in Special Operations to recover the injured and dead from civilian (Empire Portia) and military vessels (HMS *Fury*, HMS *Rodney*, and torpedo boat destroyers) that had been bombed in the Channel by the German Luftwaffe. This also included the recovery of RAF pilots who had bailed out of their aircraft, along with the recovery of intelligence papers from military personnel who were found injured, floating

Above left: John Sneath, 1927.

Above right: John pictured at home 1944, on leave from his special operations duties in.

and/or drowned at sea. The recovery of these bodies necessitated trips back to Portsmouth for an onward journey to Haslar Hospital, Gosport.

Always a lover of the outdoors, Mac enjoyed motorbike scrambles, marathon running and boating on the River Nene. He was a member of Stamford Motorcycle Club, a founder member of Peterborough Rowing Club, and president of the Peterborough Athletics Club. In the 1950s and 1960s Mac helped organise the annual round-the-city race and local athletics events. He adored the local countryside, especially the villages that formed the Soke of Peterborough, and ensured that his two daughters were familiar with the nineteenth-century poet John Clare of Helpston village.

From 1955 Mac represented Millfield on the Northamptonshire County Council (including the Soke of Peterborough) for nineteen years as a Conservative councillor. In this time he viewed politics as a way to represent and care for his local community. Always passionately interested in the Soke of Peterborough and its villages (an independent administrative county), he deeply regretted its demise – after seventy-seven years – in 1965. In Northampton he had served on committees with the 8th Earl Spencer, the father of Princess Diana.

His council committee work later led to his contribution in purchases of various artefacts for the Cromwell Museum, Huntingdon. During his nineteen years as a councillor he helped set up links to enable Peterborough to be twinned with Bourges in France; a plaque depicting the Bourges coat of arms can be seen on the east side of the Peterborough's seventeenth-century Guildhall in Cathedral Square. He was an avid researcher of both family and local history, to the extent that Fenland author and poet Edward Storey described him as a 'true Peterborian' – a personal tribute to the service he gave to his local community and to the county and Soke of Peterborough. In later years he retained his sense of humour and greatly enjoyed being a grandfather.

Mac died peacefully at his home in Eye on 28 March 1987, aged seventy-eight. Despite suffering from arthritis he remained fit to the day of his death, cycling the 10-mile round trip from his home to the Peterborough Conservative Club where he was a trustee for over thirty-five years.

21. Norman Cross, the First POW Camp

The site of Norman Cross POW camp was a 40-acre field, purchased by the government in 1796. Its prisoners were captured mainly in naval engagements and held captive in the only purpose-built POW camp in England at that time.

Five hundred carpenters and labourers erected what was considered to be permanent buildings. Around thirty wells were sunk to draw drinking water. The barracks were designed to hold 5,000–6,000 prisoners, who were mostly marched to the prison four abreast, although some were loaded into barges at King's Lynn and brought up the River Nene to Peterborough's quayside.

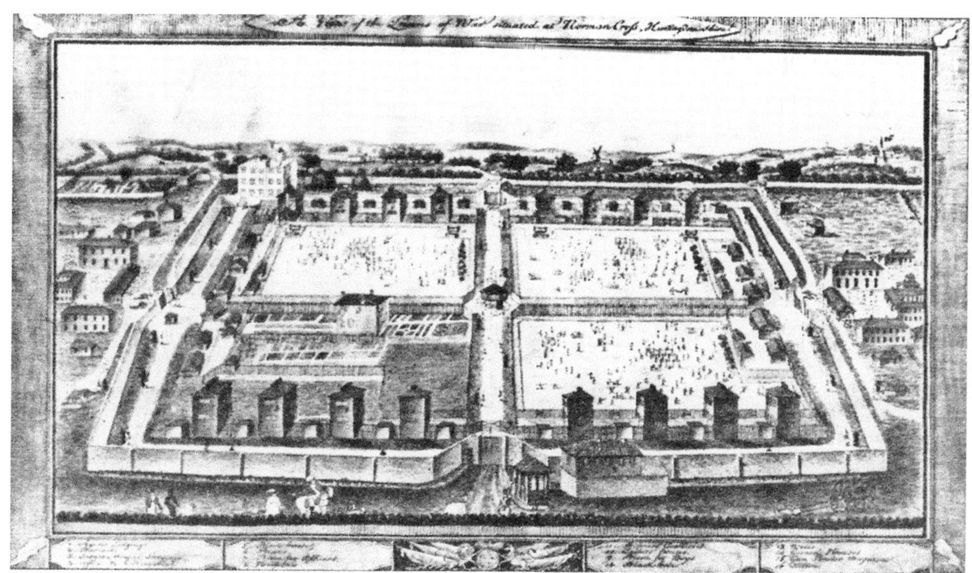

An 1810 sketch of the camp.

Prisoners in the Norman Cross depot included ex-soldiers and sailors from France, Holland, Spain, Italy and German states allied to France; a small number of women who followed their men into captivity; boys aged as young as twelve; plus many civilians from merchant vessels and government offices in enemy colonies captured by British forces.

Setbacks in the prison emerged early in the summer of 1797, when countless numbers of local people and those from further afield visited the prisoners. The guards found it hard to control these crowds as well as observe the prisoners. Finally, many visitors were stopped from entering the compounds unless accompanied by military staff. In 1797 two French prisoners took advantage of the confusion and made their escape, but only got as far as Wisbech before they were recaptured. A French officer escaped in the winter of 1797 but was never caught.

By 1800 the conditions in the prison had dramatically deteriorated and many prominent people in London, as well as locals, expressed their deep concern. In 1801, the British government issued statements blaming the French consul for not supplying sufficient clothing (the British government had paid the French for all English prisoners held in France and its colonies to be clothed). However, the French prisoners were accused by

DID YOU KNOW ?

The renowned Doctor Samuel Johnson and a Mr Serle, who visited the barracks, compiled a report on behalf of the British government, stating that the proportion of food allowance was fully sufficient to maintain both life and health, but added: 'provided it is not shamefully lost by gambling.' The Lords of the Admiralty, along with Doctor Johnson, instructed that naked prisoners should be clothed at once, without waiting for the French supply or payment for clothing.

A spectacular palace made entirely from wood and bone with clockwork and water-powered mechanisms, including a rotating waterwheel and many moving figures. From the Norman Cross exhibition at the city museum. (Courtesy of Peterborough Museum & Art Gallery)

the British government of selling their clothes and minimal personal possessions to raise money for betting.

In April 1801 six prisoners escaped Norman Cross. Three of them were caught at Boston and the remainder were caught in a fishing boat off the Norfolk coast.

Each year the attempts to escape intensified, as did the numbers in each endeavour, the latter reflecting the increased prison population. Records show that in July 1804 around 1,600 prisoners were held at the barracks; by October 1804 the figure had risen to 3,300.

Insubordination was commonplace among prisoners and escapes continued. In 1804, it was discovered that the prisoners had taken to forgery. Engraved plates and various printing implements of a very high calibre were found, both enabling the forging of bank notes. Some inmates occupied themselves by making bone (saved from their meal rations) and wood models of ships or anything else that captured their imagination. A wonderful collection of these magnificent bone and wood artefacts can be seen today at Peterborough Museum.

In January 1812 a French prisoner was shot dead while escaping after he had overpowered a guard and stolen a bayonet, and during August 1813 some escaped prisoners from Norman Cross were discovered in distant Hampshire.

Peace was proclaimed in 1814 following Napoleon's defeat and resulting abdication. All the prisoners and the garrison guards had left Norman Cross by June 1814 and two years later the buildings were demolished. Several were purchased and reassembled as dwelling houses in Peterborough.

Unveiling of the memorial on Tuesday 28 July 1914.

DID YOU KNOW ?

A memorial to the 1,700 men whose bodies were interred between 1797 and 1814 deep within the fields of Norman Cross was purchased at a cost of £200 and erected in 1914 by the Entente Cordiale Society. It had an eagle perched on a column that was said to be 'French in character ... not in an attitude of defiance, but mournful, sorrowful'. The eagle was stolen in 1990 and its replacement was unveiled on 2 April 2005.

22. Nutts about Horses

Thomas Nutt was born in Uppingham in 1852 and married Elizabeth Henson (aged twenty) in 1875 at Crowland Abbey where her parents, William Thomas Henson and Ann Eliza (née Slator), were also married.

The census of 1881 shows Thomas and Elizabeth Nutt living at No. 8 Double Row, Boongate (now Eastgate). The entry is as follows:

Thomas NUTT, head, aged 29, Horse Dealer, born Uppingham
Elizabeth Rebecca NUTT, wife aged 26, born Crowland
William Robert NUTT, son aged 5, born Peterborough
George NUTT, son aged 4, born Peterborough

Thomas NUTT, son aged 2, born Peterborough
Harry Henson NUTT, son aged 9 months, born Peterborough died 1884
Joseph BURTON, visitor, aged 30, Horse Dealer, born Spalding.

DID YOU KNOW ?

Thomas and Elizabeth had substantial stables in Eastgate and lived in an imposing three-storey residence called Rutland House on Star Road. The then Earl Fitzwilliam was known to buy several hunting horses from their stable yard.

When Thomas died at the age of forty-five in 1897 his wife Elizabeth (aged forty-two) was left with eleven children to support. Elizabeth successfully retained control of the horse-breeding and dealer's business and later married Joseph Burton who was their business manager. By all accounts Elizabeth was a very shrewd business woman, a keen politician, and a successful and charitable woman.

Both Elizabeth and Joseph were staunch Liberal activists and Elizabeth ensured that they canvassed everyone that was eligible to vote in the Boongate area to return a Liberal MP to Peterborough and a Liberal city councillor for the ward. Elizabeth used to take beer out to the Irish labourers working on building the roads in Boongate. This was all part and parcel of ensuring that they were registered to vote and could support the Liberal Party.

Sadly, Elizabeth was diagnosed with cancer in 1920 and eventually died two years later of pneumonia at the age of sixty-five.

Thomas and Elizabeth Nutt's third eldest son also called Thomas, known as Tom, went to Brussels in 1900 and was a respected horse dealer, becoming a contact between Europe

Stables in Eastgate.

Rutland House, Eastgate.

and the Nutt family in Peterborough. He became a part of the huge fraternity of renowned horse dealers. Tom apparently used to come over to the International Horse show at Olympia, London, and rode there before the outbreak of the First World War.

Elizabeth's son also played a part in the 1912 King George V Gold Cup at the International Horse Jumping Show, which was won by a horse called 'Murat' and ridden by Lieutenant Delvoie of Belgium (who became the Belgian military attaché to Paris during the First World War). Tom was said to be either the horse's trainer or owner at that time.

Elizabeth Nutt, 1904.

DID YOU KNOW ?
The successful horse dealership ended in 1951, nearly eighty years on from when Thomas and Elizabeth started to build up an honest dealing business in Peterborough – then a small cathedral city known throughout the Midlands as a town of 'Pride, Poverty, Parsons and Pubs'.

23. Agent Q

Born in London in July 1864, Le Queux (pronounced 'Q'), was one of the first to exploit the potential of technology in his spy thrillers. In fact, William's story *The Invasion* (1906) caused such a stir in Edwardian society that some people started to report all sorts of strange happenings and likely suspicious people to the police.

A self-proclaimed secret agent, William became 'the master of mystery', credited by some with creating the prototype of 007 and managing to outsell the works of Edgar Wallace and John Buchan.

DID YOU KNOW ?
In 1900, Le Queux rented The Cedars, No. 32 Peterborough Road, Castor, for four years where he wrote over fifty books.

The Cedars, Castor.

William was the son of a draper's assistant and born in Walworth, London, in 1864. He soon left his working-class roots behind and set off to study in Italy and Paris before beginning a career in journalism. He initially worked for *The Globe* (founded in 1803), a British newspaper that merged with the *Pall Mall Gazette* in 1921. While a journalist at *The Globe* in the 1890s, he reported on the first Balkan War and thereafter took up writing books on a professional basis.

William was also a diplomat, explorer, and a flying buff, who in 1909 officiated at the first air meeting in Britain. He was also a wireless pioneer who broadcast music from his own station long before radio was generally available. He formed a friendship with John Logie Baird (the Scottish engineer and inventor of the world's first working television).

William wrote in the genres of mystery, thriller and espionage in the years leading up to the First World War. His friendship with British publishing magnate Lord Alfred Northcliffe led to the serialised publication of pulp-fiction spy stories like *The Invasion of 1910, The Poisoned Bullet,* and *Spies of the Kaiser.* These stories were examples of invasion literature, a common phenomenon prior to the First World War in Europe, involving fictionalised stories of potential invasion or penetration by foreign powers. William's specialty was the German invasion of Great Britain and he was also the original editor of Lord Northcliffe's *War of the Nations.* Lord Northcliffe was the founder of *The Daily Mail* (1896) and *The Mirror* (1903) and later he bought *The Times* in 1908.

Was William Le Queux the first 007? Well, let's examine the evidence. One of his characters, a spy called Duckworth Drew, is said to have provided the inspiration for Ian

A 1914 Le Queux book cover.

Fleming's fictional creation, James Bond. There are several coincidences (or clues) here: William Le Queux's surname is pronounced 'Q'; the hero is a gentleman and a womaniser; he works for the Marquis of Macclesfield, known as M; two Le Queux novels feature Bond in the titles *Guilty Bonds, Bond of Black* and *The Man With The Fatal Finger* – a cross between *The Man with the Golden Gun* and *Goldfinger*

In the years before the First World War, William's novels warned that Britain was under assault from 'a vast army of German spies' and his book *The Invasion of 1910* (1906) sold more than a million copies. The British Secret Service Bureau (later split into MI5 and MI6) was founded in 1909, to some extent in response to William's scaremongering and the public's reaction to it. Yet, as Christopher Andrew reveals in his history of MI5, there was a German espionage network operating in Britain before the First World War, so, in the characteristics of cheap fiction and public anxiety, lay nuggets of fact.

DID YOU KNOW ?

Le Queux lived in Italy for a while and was made a consul under the Italian government. In 1906, he was made a Cavalier (Knight) of the Order of San Marino.

Just imagine, the original Q lived on the doorsteps of Peterborough and in 1914 Peterborough had to have the Riot Act read because of the anti-German feeling that led to violence in the city centre.

Like his fictional character Monsieur Raoul Becq, Le Queux died in Belgium in October 1927. He was an ardent student of human nature, a student who studied and wrote about some of the most fascinating and infamous criminals of his day. Although Le Queux is no longer highly regarded as an author of crime fiction, he continues to be recognised as an influential figure in the development of the spy novel.

24. Worlidge – Peterborough's Rembrandt

Thomas was born in Peterborough in 1700, the son of Richard Worlidge. Two of Thomas' brothers and his sister are entered in the parish register of St John the Baptist Church.

Thomas is best remembered as an early Rembrandtist, imitating the drypoint style of the master and making direct copies of famous prints and producing compositions of his own 'after the manner of Rembrandt'.

He took drawing lessons from the Italian painter Alessandro Maria Grimaldi (1659–1732), and went to Birmingham in around 1736 with Grimaldi's son Alexander (1714–1800) where he worked as a glass painter.

Above left: A Thomas Worlidge sketch in the style of Rembrandt.

Above right: Self-portrait, dated 1754.

Thomas married Grimaldi's daughter, Arabella, and the couple moved to London in the mid-1730s. They initially lived in Covent Garden and while there Thomas became acquainted with the engraver Louis Pierre Boitard. Perhaps because of his closeness to the London theatres, Thomas' early works were mainly portraits of actors and theatregoers. He made a drawing on vellum of Theophilus Cibber (1735), a painting of David Garrick as Tancred (*c.* 1745) and a miniature of the mimic Samuel Foote. Thomas' watercolour of the comic actress Kitty Clive as the Fine Lady in Garrick's *Lethe* was copied for a Bow porcelain figurine in around 1750–52.

In the 1750s and 1760s Thomas worked in Bath and its surrounding area drawing and painting portraits in miniature, pencil, crayon and oil. His most popular works were portrait heads in pencil, which were in great demand by fashionable Bath socialites. Thomas exhibited at the Society of Artists in 1761 and 1765 and at the Free Society in 1762 and 1765–66 and he is recognised as having been the single most active figure in the Rembrandt revival in eighteenth-century England.

As the British School of Painting emerged in the eighteenth century, copies of Old Master paintings were highly sought after by artists who had very few British works to refer to as exemplars. It is likely that Thomas Gainsborough, William Hoare and Thomas Barker were introduced to Rembrandt's work through Thomas Worlidge's copies.

One of Thomas' many achievements is the reintroduction into England of the art of painting on glass, painted miniature portraits, and etchings of antiquities. He died in Hammersmith, London, on 22 September 1766, aged sixty-six.

25. A Discovery of Gold, Diamonds and Alum

Leading Brazilian newspaper *A Tarde* published an article on 26 April 1922 about a Peterborian named Herbert Waite. He was the son of Thomas Waite of No. 184 Lincoln Road and had started his journey to Bahia State (north-east Brazil on the Atlantic coast) in November 1920 as a land surveyor. Some eighteen months later Herbert Waite had discovered a pure alum (double sulphate salts) mine in the Sincora Mountain of central Bahia. The discovery of this mine made it the largest of its kind at that time. The mine covered over 40 kilometres and was part-owned by Herbert Waite and the French millionaire Marcel Bouilloux-Lafont (1871–1944), a banker and industrialist.

The newspaper article recounted a thrilling story about Mr Waite's journey into the interior of north-east Brazil to conduct his survey. He writes from Jiquy on 10 April 1922 to say:

> Here I am right in the centre of the great gold and diamond field of Bahia State. Last night I was lulled to sleep by the roaring of the tigers in the hills. I am stuck here for fresh horses and shall not get away until tomorrow. The climate is wonderful at 1,950 feet above sea level. Iracema (now named Almas) I passed on the train to here is 2,500 feet above sea level and for 10 miles either side it runs through a dense forest in which the trees surpass in height anything I could have imagined. The forest is just a closed wall of trees of all sizes, of wonderful grandeur and full of fearsome possibilities as regards snakes and wildlife. Tomorrow I start for Passaqau Joad Manoel – some 25 miles on horseback – an ordeal I am not looking forward to, as the road passes over crags. But beneath these crags is an endless wealth of gold and diamonds. Huge fortunes are made weekly in this district. I can actually see the sun shining on that wall of alum in the famous Serra do Sincora mountains!

Alum mining, *c.* 1920.

Sincora mountains in Bahia State, Brazil.

Writing to his friend Charles Hughes on 20 April 1922, he says:

> Here I am in Passaqua Joad Manoel, 4,200 feet above sea level. Here amid the snakes, tigers, wild cats and every other nuisance of the animal and insect world, not excluding the horrid 'garrapatas' [ticks] which invade one's leggings and shins and leave septic sores by the score. We cut our way through the 24 miles of virgin forest up to the great wall of alum. Practically pure alum is present in deposits of millions of tons - 40 square kilometres of it!

Herbert Waite left England in late 1920 to take up the post of chief resident engineer of Brazil's South-Western Railway. He relinquished this position as soon as he discovered huge deposits of alum and having panned successfully for deposits of gold and diamonds.

DID YOU KNOW ?

Herbert Tom Waite married Mamoela Gonçalez (a Spanish lady) in Brazil and had a brother named Reginald who remained in Peterborough. Herbert's granddaughter Claudia Waite de Souza still lives in Brazil and is a government lawyer. Claudia would like to know more about her family here in Peterborough, so if you can add to this story please get in touch.

26. Peterborough's Banana King

George Meadows was a businessman and exotic fruit entrepreneur. He was born on 8 January 1860 in Werrington, Peterborough. It seems that on leaving school George went to work as an apprentice grocer in London. He then became a travelling grocer's assistant until he married Elizabeth Jervis on 4 May 1884. They set up shop in March (then part of the Isle of Ely) and in the 1891 census they lived at Broad Street, March, with George's occupation being listed as a grocer.

In 1898, George's home address was No. 22 Craig Terrace, Peterborough, and he opened his first shop in Cowgate (between Edwin Davis and the Bridge Café). Sadly, his wife Elizabeth died aged thirty-five, on 30 August 1900. The obituary shows the family living at No. 41 Lincoln Road. The 1901 census records show that he is a widower and living with four children and his mother-in-law.

George, however, was not to be alone for long, as on 30 April 1908 he married the twenty-three-year-old Jane Perkins Letch of Dogsthorpe. George was aged forty-eight when he married Jane, his shop assistant and twenty-five years his junior. They went on to have a son. Philip George Perkins Meadows was born on 31 May 1909 at No. 24 Cowgate.

In 1926, George had shops in Lincoln Road, Cowgate and Broad Bridge Street and added the warehouses in Geneva Street to his property portfolio.

In December 1926 George bought the warehouse at No. 66 Westgate for £900 from George Frederick Rippon of Queen Street. The premises were installed with six air-tight thermal rooms

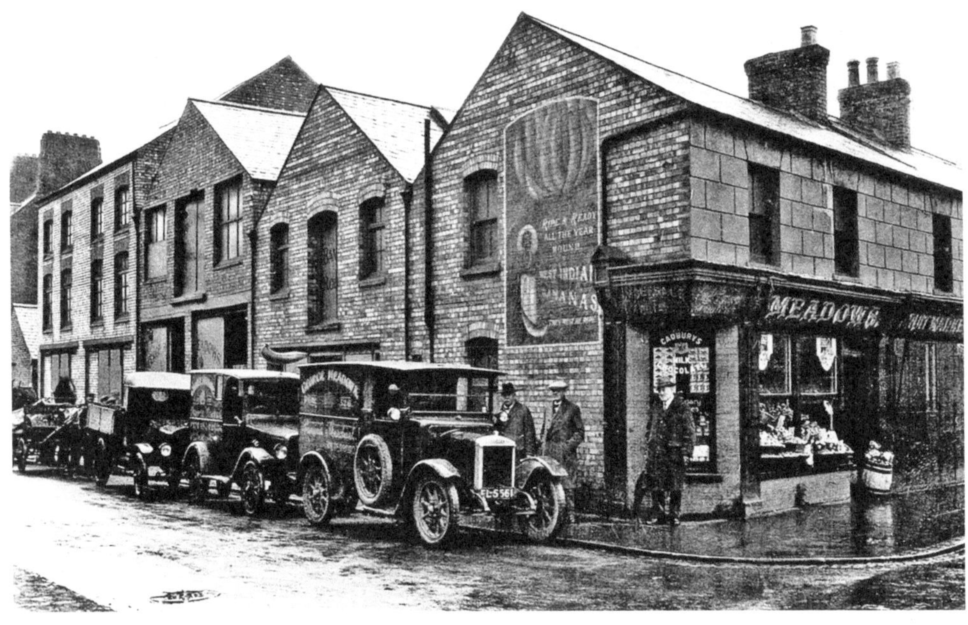

Shop at the corner of Lincoln Road and Geneva Street, *c.* 1928.

Shop at No. 66 Westgate, *c.* 1931.

to ripen the bananas (imported from the West Indies, Canary Islands, and elsewhere), and it was thought in 1927 that this property had the most up-to-date thermal chambers in Britain.

The banana rooms at No. 66 Westgate were built by James Moore of Hull at a cost of £596. In 1969, there was an explosion causing fatalities at the Westgate warehouse.

George Meadows introduced Canary bananas (then an exotic fruit) to the city's marketplace in the Victorian period and it was said that he had to show local people how to peel and eat this unfamiliar but colourful fruit. Some were a little reluctant at first, but soon grew to like this nutritional fruit that came complete with its own packaging. It is thought by some scientists that the banana is the oldest fruit in the world.

Peterborough's 'Banana King' died peacefully aged seventy-two at his home at No. 21 Cowgate on 18 December 1932.

27. The Pocket Hercules

Francis 'Frank' Buckle was born the son of a saddler in Newmarket in 1767. Originally the Buckle family came from Westmoreland. Sadly, his father died when he was aged twelve and an aunt brought him up. Fortunately, Frank saw no future in saddlery and became an apprentice to Richard Vernon, who noticed and developed Buckle's riding skills. Shortly after this Frank became the favoured jockey for Sir Charles Bunbury, Colonel Mellish, as well as the stable jockey at the Grafton stables.

DID YOU KNOW ?
Frank was one of the early leading jockeys, weighing only 3st 13lbs when he first started riding. He was known as the 'Pocket Hercules' because of his handling of horses at speed and his tiny stature.

As a sixteen-year-old, Frank walked out Mr Richard Vernon's horse 'Wolf' at Newmarket, and in 1783, aged seventeen, he made his first race appearance. Some seven years later he won both the St Leger Stakes and the Epsom Derby on 'Champion'. Frank rode twenty-seven Classics including five Derby winners, nine Epsom Oaks winners and two St Leger stakes winners. His most impressive performance came when he rode 'Hambletonian' against 'Diamond' at Newmarket in 1799. Frank's championship record was not beaten until the arrival of Lester Piggott, who won his first race in 1954. Frank had held the record for well over 120 years.

During the 1790s Frank remained as light as a feather at a weight of only 3st 13lb, but at the turn of the 1800s his riding weight increased to 8st 7lb, which he maintained with ease. It was said of Frank Buckle that 'there was nothing flash or big about him, except his heart and nose'. At a time when jockeys were permitted to bet, Buckle often rode against his own financial interest and was deemed a rare man of principle and reliability, which was against the norm in the late eighteenth century, when jockeys were mainly corrupt and often violent types.

DID YOU KNOW ?
Frank was highly regarded by fellow jockeys for his stamina and sheer determination to win. The public also took to him because of his utter honesty and simplicity of character. He was a much-loved jockey and a bit of a celebrity, long before racing became fashionable for the masses.

Champion jockey Frank Buckle.

Buckle's farm, now the Botolph Arms.

He lived on his farm at Botolph in Orton Longueville, Peterborough, and apparently made the 92-mile round trip to Newmarket, returning home daily by 6 p.m. after a day's riding at the races. Frank is buried at Holy Trinity church, Orton Longueville and continued riding until his death at the age of sixty-five in 1832.

The Botolph Arms pub is thought to be the farm Frank owned, which at the time had substantial fields attached to it. Today, Frank's sarcophagus can be located within the burial grounds of Trinity Church, but it looks rather neglected and overgrown with ivy.

28. RAF Peterborough (Westwood Airfield)

RAF Westwood opened in 1932 and served as a training base for Allied & Commonwealth pilots throughout the war and early post-war years. Aircraft flown included Tutors, Harts, Audax, Fury, Demon, Battles, Moths, Oxfords, Masters, Ansons, Hurricanes and Harvards.

In 1948, the Ministry placed the airfield under 'civil care and maintenance' and for two years British Airways used it as a helicopter base for regular airmail services for East Anglia, with the General Post Office sorting the mail and parcels in aircraft hangars.

DID YOU KNOW ?

From 1958 to 1963 (the airfield closed in 1964), Baker Perkins, Mitchell Engineering and Mitchell Construction used part of the airfield to house their company aircraft.

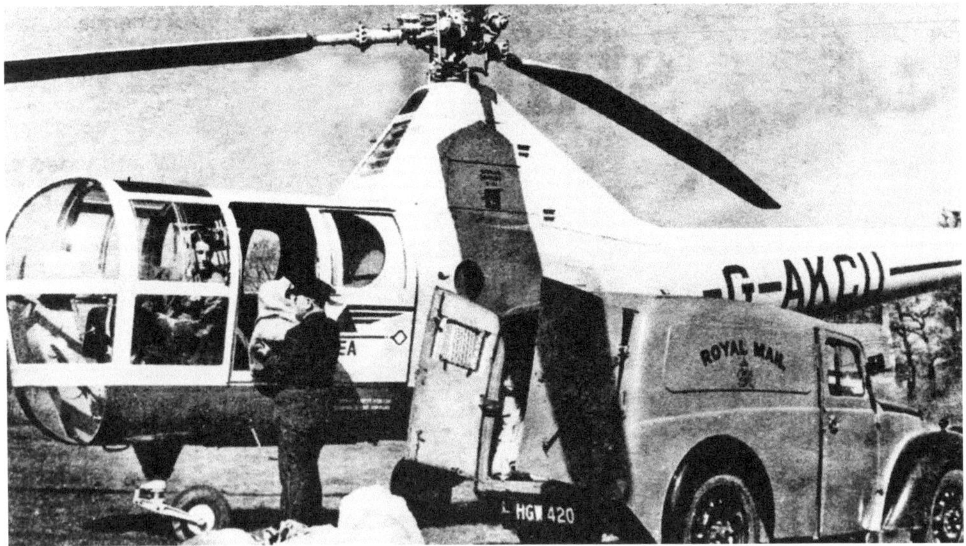

Helicopter airmail service.

The Station Office (No. 5) in Saville Road is one of only three remaining brick-built station buildings and is unique as a distinctive and important military building. It is a two-storey dark-red brick building under a slate roof. The main entrance has a pillastered door case. The Sergeants' Mess, also located in Saville Road, is a tall single dark-red brick building with a slate roof.

However, the jewel in the crown is the remaining Junior Officers Quarters and Mess, in Cottesmore Close. It is a commanding building in a formal and uniform style. The two-storey dark-red brick building is under a slate roof with slightly projecting eaves. The main entrance comprises a white painted stucco portico with four columns. The building is set within a driveway with railings defining the boundary.

Runway approach, with the runway on the left.

The airbase was not without its fair share of flying accidents. The most significant was on 16 April 1936, when the newly arrived twenty-year-old Air Cadet Harold Eric Smith-Langridge was killed along with the thirty-six-year-old pilot Flight Lieutenant Ernest Dawson in their dual-controlled Hawker Hart. Their aircraft was performing its second loop at 300 feet and suddenly it hit the ground, crashing into a hangar after flying in formation with two other aircraft. Two RAF personnel on the ground were also killed when struck by the aircraft, namely Percy Cuthbert and Stanley King (who died the following day). It seems the fire also destroyed an Avro Tutor and three Audax aeroplanes. The court of inquiry stated that the probable cause of the crash was due to the pilot, Flight Lieutenant Dawson, being drunk.

Another fatality was that of William Dycer Coppinger, who was killed in an air accident on 23 October 1936.

From 1964 much of the airfield had residential homes built on it and today most of the site is part of Netherton and Westwood housing estates. All that remains today is the Junior Officers Quarters and Mess in Cottesmore Close. Presently, RAF Westwood is the home to Royal Air Force Cadet Squadron 115 Air Training Corp, in Saville Road. Their motto is 'to Aspire, Achieve and Excel in everything they do'.

RAF station buildings in the foreground.

29. J. Arthur Rank Organisation and Percussionist James Blades OBE

James was born on 9 September 1901 at No. 6 Albert Place, Peterborough, and lived with his parents, grandparents, a cousin and three brothers. From a very early age he fell in love with drumming while watching a member of the Salvation Army banging a bass drum. By the time he was eleven he had shown an aptitude for playing the drum in the boy scouts and kept his musical interests wide by singing in Peterborough Cathedral choir, the music of Tallis, Byrd and the then modern composer John Stainer. Decades later James met two of Peterborough Cathedral's former senior choristers, namely Malcolm Sargent and Thomas Armstrong in other musical arenas.

DID YOU KNOW ?

James had a promising early career as an engineer but bouts of depression meant he left school at the age of thirteen rather than fourteen. He decided to receive drum lessons from his Uncle George, who was fond of beating his knife and fork on the dinner table, and from then on James was obsessed with drums. When he was fourteen he joined a circus in Wisbech in which he played the cymbals and a bass drum, providing the beat for a dancing elephant.

James began performing in local Peterborough bands and dropped his apprenticeship in engineering. He spent most of the 1920s working at local movie theatres, creating sound effects for silent movies and then playing in dance bands around Britain.

In 1932, he joined the London Film Society Orchestra and in 1935 created the sound of the gong at the beginning of movies made by J. Arthur Rank Studios. James' recording was mimed by a boxer, William Thomas Wells (better known as Bombardier Billy Wells).

The most notable sound James made was the dot-dot-dot-dash ditty of 'V-for-victory' Morse code that the BBC broadcast to encourage the Resistance in continental Europe during the Second World War. This recording transmitted 150 times a day from 1940 to 1945 and echoed the da-da-da-dum phrase that begins Beethoven's *Fifth Symphony*. To create the signal James used a tympani mallet to strike an African membrane drum, essentially a tom-tom with the sound damped with a handkerchief.

Shortly after the war, in 1945, his wife Olive Hewitt died but his broadcasting, commercial and film work continued at a rate of knots. In 1948 he married oboist Joan Goossens and with this marriage came a new career opportunity for James. Joan suggested the idea of lecturing, and it is through this avenue of work that James is most fondly remembered by generations of 1950s schoolchildren, industrial workers,

Right: James Blades.

Below: James Blades' autograph, 1972.

With every good wish
James Blades
8/1/72

prison inmates, the disabled, music club members and early television viewers. These lecture/recital demonstrations with Joan affected thousands, not only because of his mastery of percussion but also through his charm, wit, wisdom, and the wonder of his talent. James died on 19 May 1999 aged ninety-seven at his home at No. 191 Sandy Lane, Cheam, Surrey.

DID YOU KNOW ?

In 1954, James was appointed a professor of percussion at the Royal Academy of Music and in 1972 he was awarded an OBE.

30. Arthur John Rowledge MBE, FRS

Arthur John Rowledge was born at No. 47 Gladstone Street, Peterborough, in 1876, the son of John and Ann Rowledge.

DID YOU KNOW ?
Arthur's father, John, had a small building business that had been inherited from his grandfather, who apparently helped to build Crystal Palace.

In his early boyhood Arthur spent time at his maternal grandfather's farm in Whaplode, Lincolnshire. His grandfather got Arthur interested in sketching and the arts and explained a lot of scientific and mechanical things so that as a young boy he knew how the steam engine worked.

Arthur attended St Peter's College, Peterborough, when Mr Seabrook was headmaster. The college also had a school of science and art situated in the cathedral precincts. Arthur attended both while a student at St Peter's, as well as during his apprenticeship with Barford & Perkins Engineers in Queen Street (the site is now part of Queensgate shopping complex). John Edward Sharman Perkins (father of Frank Perkins) was the works manager at Barford & Perkins and he taught Arthur a lot about the workings of the foundry.

DID YOU KNOW ?
Arthur went on to design the Napier Lion aero engine and was a vital figure in the development of the limited Rolls-Royce Merlin engine.

Arthur joined Napier & Son in 1913 as chief designer. After designing car engines and the Napier Lion aero engine, Arthur took up a position at Rolls Royce Ltd in 1921, where, in the company's shorthand, he became known as 'Rg' – an abridgement of Rowledge.

In June 1914 Arthur patented a way of starting the internal combustion engine of a Wolseley car, and some five years later he took out a patent for a car cylinder as well as a patent for a fluid tight socket/plug for a car engine. On 26 March 1920 Arthur was awarded the MBE for his work as chief designer at Napier & Son Ltd.

Nearly a decade later Arthur is credited with designing the Condor III, Kestrel and the Rolls-Royce R racing engines, all of which were used with resounding success at the 1929 and 1931 Schneider Trophy races. It was the Schneider Trophy Contest that Great Britain won outright to retain the trophy in perpetuity by winning the air race three times consecutively in 1927, 1929 and 1931.

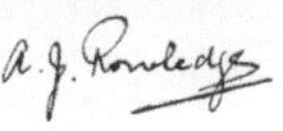

Signed image of Arthur Rowledge.

Postcard of the Supermarine Rolls-Royce Monoplane.

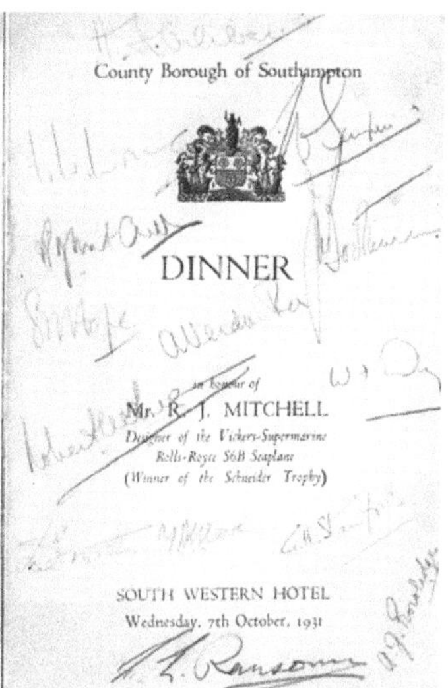

County Borough of Southampton

DINNER

in honour of

Mr. R. J. MITCHELL

Designer of the Vickers-Supermarine Rolls-Royce S6B Seaplane (Winner of the Schneider Trophy)

SOUTH WESTERN HOTEL

Wednesday, 7th October, 1931

Autographed menu from 1931.

The 1931 win was mainly due to Reginald Mitchell, an aircraft designer who designed the Spitfire; Arthur Rowledge, the Rolls-Royce engine designer; and Flight Lieutenant John Boothman, who was the Vickers-Supermarine S6B seaplane pilot.

In 1941 Arthur was made a fellow of the Royal Society for the Improvement of Natural Knowledge.

It is perhaps the development work he did on the Rolls-Royce Merlin engine that Arthur remains best known for, along with his contributions to advancement of aero engine design. He retired from Rolls-Royce at the age of seventy in 1945. Arthur died at Derby on 11 December 1957, aged eighty-one.

31. Royal Visits and the King's Lodging

In the first seven centuries of Peterborough's ecclesiastical history, ten kings visited the abbey church. From King Stephen onwards, they came mostly to venerate the holy relic of St Oswald's arm, which was preserved in the altar of one of the chapels in the south transept.

Firstly came Peada, the first Christian King of Mercia, who in AD 655 built the original monastery at Medeshamstede, 'laying such stones in the foundations that eight yoke of oxen could scarcely carry one of them'. He was succeeded by King Wolfhere, his brother, who continued to build the monastery, getting his stone from the nearby quarries at Barnack. A younger brother, Etheldred, succeeded him and built the abbot's house, which is still in use as part of the Bishop's Palace.

The fourth king to visit Medeshamstede was Edgar in 970, who had caused a second church to be built to replace the original one destroyed by the Danes a century before. He had the town's name changed to Burgh.

DID YOU KNOW ?

In around 1070 King Canute and his queen, Emma, visited the monastery and were presented with richly worked manuscripts. It is recorded that they were caught in a heavy storm while sailing on the vast lake of Whittlesea (Whittlesey) Mere and were in danger of shipwreck. Canute shortly afterwards caused a dike to be cut from Peterborough in the direction of Whittlesey and Ramsey, known as the King's Delph.

King Stephen was entertained in around 1150 by Abbot Martin de Vecti when he came to venerate the sacred relics collected by the earlier abbot, Elsinus, including the arm of St Oswald.

King John did not come to worship but probably visited the monastery in 1215 during his church-plundering campaign. This campaign produced much of the treasures later lost in the Wash.

Abbot Walter of Peterborough entertained Henry III so well on 28 February 1234 that he returned later with his queen and the young prince.

King Canute.

Edward I and his queen came in around 1300 and were given hospitality by Abbot Godfrey of Croyland (Crowland). Later, Prince Edward and his favourite – Piers Gaveston – visited the abbot and were each presented with an equivalent value of rich robes.

The last recorded medieval visit by a monarch was in 1327 when Edward III was sumptuously received by Abbot Adam de Boothby. Later, his son Edward the Black Prince, with his sisters and servants, were hospitably treated at the abbey for eight weeks.

Throughout the centuries the abbot was the chief local citizen, being not only the head of the monastery but the equivalent of the present-day lord lieutenant, chief magistrate and head of all local administration. It was the dean of the cathedral (abbey church) who inherited many of these functions right up to 1874.

Built in around 1175, the King's Lodgings, which adjoins the right of the Norman archway (St Nicholas Gateway) leading to the cathedral precincts was used in the Middle Ages as a dwelling for the king, his family and other important royal officials. From 655 to 1327, kings came mostly to venerate the holy relic of St Oswald's arm, so the lodgings would have been their main residence.

After this period the King's Lodgings was converted to a courthouse and used by the abbot's justices. Subsequently it was used as the town's gaol.

DID YOU KNOW ?

During 1334 the king's Lodgings suffered damage and the only surviving part is that which exists today.

When used as a gaol, the larger room of the lodgings had a wooden enclosure to secure the prisoners. This enclosed space was subdivided into two cells. Between these cells and the St Nicholas Gateway was the gaol room, or condemned cell, which had no light because its twelfth-century window had been blocked off and only the iron-grated opening (10 inches by 7 inches) in the door provided light and air.

The upstairs room was used as a prison for debtors. According to Dr Lettson, who inspected and reported on the gaol in 1805: 'Debtors have a spacious good room upstairs and if the keeper furnishes bed, they pay 2 shillings and 4d a week. They have no allowance, no employment provided for any. The gaol is very clean.'

From 1576 Elizabeth I's treasurer, William, Lord Burghley, and his descendants the earls and marquesses of Exeter became responsible for the maintenance of the King's Lodgings (then the liberty gaol) until a new gaol was built in Thorpe Road (the Sessions House) to replace it and the house of correction in Cumbergate. To this day inmates' etchings mark the building's walls.

Around the same time as the Guildhall was being restored in 1928/29 the King's Lodgings was also reordered back to its original state. The window that had been blocked up was opened out again and the wooden door was resited to its original location.

Today a small plaque relating to the mullioned wooden door reads: 'This door was preserved for many years by the Peterborough Natural History and Archaeological Society in its museum, and was in the year 1930 given by the Society to be rehung here, its original position, and there to remain.'

DID YOU KNOW ?

After the King's Lodgings was restored in 1929 it opened as a pharmacy. A few years after that it became a SPCK Christian bookshop and then in September 1995 it opened as Balagan (a bespoke gift shop), and later as Reba Boutique (part of Balagan) on a lease from Peterborough City Council. Today it is a MAGPAS Air Ambulance charity shop.

King's Lodgings as a pharmacy.

32. Special Operations Executive (SOE) and the Fighting Jedburghs at Orton Hall

Orton Hall was requisitioned by the army in 1940 and the grounds were used as a battle training area with tracked vehicles cutting up the grassland etc. Later during the Second World War, some volunteers recruited from the armed forces of Britain, America and France with a small contingent from the Netherlands, Belgium and Canada named the Jedburghs set up a home base at Milton Hall, near Peterborough. There in 1944 they undertook months of exhaustive training, covering all aspects of guerrilla warfare, ambushes, demolition, unarmed combat, silent killing, parachuting and the techniques of reception committee work for receiving additional supplies by air when operating behind enemy lines. Some moved from Milton Hall to Orton Hall to refine their guerrilla and espionage skills.

The latter was important because Jedburgh teams, of mostly three people from nearly 300 recruits, carried out over 100 operations in Europe – ninety-three were with the Marquis in France in support of Allied landings, and eight in the Netherlands.

Later, the Jeds, as they were called, did similar operations with other Allied forces like the American Office of Strategic Services (OSS) and the British 136 Special Operations Executive (SOE) in Norway, Italy, Malaya, Borneo, Indonesia, China and Indo-China.

Team of three operatives.

Training at Milton Hall.

DID YOU KNOW ?
During the war years the cricket square near Orton Hall was fenced off and the pavilion locked for military training and other exercises. This remained the case until 1946, probably due to the Jedburgh's involvement in conflicts immediately after the Second World War.

Not all the Jedburghs returned as some were killed in action, others were executed, some died of their wounds and others of illnesses contracted on operations in the jungles of south-east Asia.

A memorial to the thirty-seven Jedburghs who died can be seen in the Sprite Chapel of Peterborough Cathedral. They include: Sergeant J. Austin, Major H. Brinkgreve, Major D. Britton, Sergeant P. Colvin, Sergeant D. Gardner, Captain V. Gough, Captain G. Marchant, Captain T. A. Mellows, Major C. Ogden-Smith, Captain J. Radice and Captain P. Vickery.

33. Sage's Factory

Frederick Sage established himself in Hatton Garden, London, in 1860 and founded the House of Frederick Sage & Co., a business that manufactured cabinets and shopfronts. A few years later his son Frederick George and his three nephews – Frederick, Josiah and Jesse Hawes – joined the company. They eventually formed a partnership with the main control in the hands of the founder.

Walton factory.

They traded worldwide and to cope with the increased volume of trade, especially from Europe, South Africa and South America, a new factory was built in 1910 at Walton in Peterborough, covering an area of 100,000 square feet.

The shopfronts and large proportion of interior shop fittings were manufactured in London and Peterborough.

Frederick Sage & Co. Ltd were not only shop fitters but makers of aeroplanes in the First World War. To meet the wartime need for seaplanes in 1915 the company was one of six selected by the Admiralty to build the Short 184 under sub-contract.

Originally twelve aircraft were ordered, but the company went on to build more than eighty Short 184s.

The Peterborough factory, conveniently located by the Great Northern mainline railway, with sidings, also used its workforce's woodworking skills to build cabins for non-rigid airships.

Not content with building aircraft on sub-contract, the company also set up an aircraft-design team, which from 1916 included the aviator and aircraft designer Eric Gordon England.

Sage Type 1 was a design for a twin-engined bomber that was not built.

Sage Type 2 was a biplane-fighter with an enclosed cockpit (first of its kind), the Admiralty ordered six but only one was built.

Sage Type 3 was a biplane-trainer also known as the Sage N3 School, 30 ordered but only two built.

Sage Type 4 was a seaplane trainer also known as the Sage N4 School, two built.

With the end of the First World War, and having built 400 planes in four years, there was a surplus of former military aircraft, so the company closed the design department and returned to wood working and shop fitting. It became involved in aircraft production again during the Second World War, building forward fuselages for Airspeed Horsa gliders. In 1942, the Minister of Aircraft Production, Sir Richard Stafford Cripps visited the factory.

After the Second World War they not only worked on shops, ships, churches, museums but their expert cabinetmakers and joiners undertook post-war work in the Palace of Westminster following the bombing of the House of Commons.

DID YOU KNOW ?

Some of Sage's interwar work included the woodwork that can be found in the interior of Peterborough Town Hall. Other prestigious installations include work for Selfridges and Harrods.

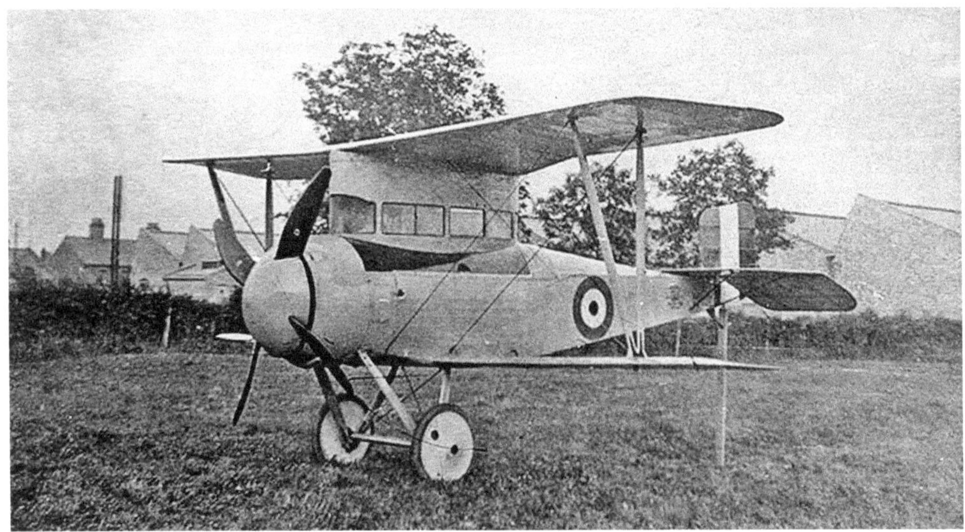

Above: Sage Type 2 with enclosed cockpit.

Left: Short 184 ready for delivery.

In 1936, the factory was taken over by Aeronica for a short while. Then in the Second World War the Walton plant became the Royal Ordnance Factory, making air-launch torpedoes. Perkins Engines used it from 1957 until 1989 when it became the Triplex Factory.

The site lay dormant for many years until the factory was demolished in the spring of 2010, except for its iconic Grade II-listed water tower. The latter is now owned by private housing developers.

34. Sheltons Bring Parisian Chic to the City

Charles William Shelton was born in 1910 and started work as a builder in Peterborough in 1931. After the Second World War his firm built the Dogsthorpe council estate as well as most of the houses in Stanground and Gunthorpe. By 1956, the company Chas Shelton Ltd was building 250 new homes a year in the area.

As Peterborough grew, Charles could see there was room for a department store and Sheltons, with its twenty-three departments selling everything from kitchens and chic fashions to food, opened in Broadway in 1962.

One of Charles' three sons, Stuart, said: 'It was just like Grace Brothers in *Are You Being Served*.' The inspiration for the store was entirely Charles', as in 1959 he bought the Theatre Royal (formerly The Empire), which brought live entertainment to Peterborough for more than seventy-five years. The theatre was demolished in 1961 to make way for Sheltons department store.

Charles Shelton's building company was responsible for the actual building and its ultra-modern design with clean lines and a predominance of glass. It was constructed in two sections and part of the store was in use while the second half was being completed.

Sheltons, Broadway.

The family owned a hardware shop and merchandise was transferred to the new premises, which opened with an impressive general stock in 1962. The store was finished in 1964 and since then was constantly developing to give a remarkably full service with the accent on high-quality goods at competitive prices. In the early 1960s the building was unique in Peterborough, having the only escalator in the city at the time. It had the distinction of including a branch of Barclays Bank within the store. The bank leased part of the ground floor with an entrance from the street and another from the store for the convenience of customers.

DID YOU KNOW ?

Among the many luxury touches to the Sheltons store were the two entrances, with the façade on the Broadway side being of Westmorland green slate with a natural ravine finish, while the entrance from Park Road was faced and polished in Vert St Denis marble quarried from the mountains of north-west Italy. The wide marble staircase leading up to the third floor was cleverly designed to give an appeal to the interior while remaining in keeping with the ultra-modern style of the store.

When Charles died in 1966 at the age of fifty-six at his home at No. 30 Westwood Park Road, his wife Laura became the chairman and managing director. She gained a vast experience in a lifetime's involvement in the retail trade. Her main interest was in clothes and she often visited fashion houses in Paris, Milan and London. Laura was more attracted to the Parisian haute couture houses and would buy the latest season's fashions as soon as the clothes went into production for the ready to wear lines. Parisian chic was her preferred style.

The couple had three sons and a daughter. Their sons Malcolm and Stuart both left school at fifteen to join their father's building business and were in on the store at the very

Staircase, *c.* 1963.

beginning. Malcolm the eldest helped to build the first stage of the store and Stuart took on the final construction and both then started work in the store. The sons shared similar interests as they both flew at the Sibson Aero Club, which was owned by the company and they piloted a light aircraft to business meetings to save time spent on crowded roads.

The store closed in 1990 as sales started to drop due to the opening of the city centre's Queensgate shopping complex in 1982, which changed everything.

In 1980, the company had opened a shop selling fishing tackle and guns. Today, Sheltons concentrates on its angling trade, operating out of its premises in South Street, Stanground. It is now one of the biggest in the region and is run by Stuart and his nephew, Charles Shelton.

35. Stargazer

George Eric Deacon Alcock MBE was the son of a self-educated railway worker. He was born in Peterborough on 28 August 1912. A bright child fascinated by insects, plants, trains and the weather. He witnessed the large partial solar eclipse of 8 April 1921 and from then on added astronomy to his many passions by observing the heavens with a small brass reflector belonging to his father.

While training to be a teacher in 1931, George joined the meteor section of the British Astronomical Association (BAA). He became one of its small team of official meteor observers with the aim of predicting optimum times for two-station observation of meteors. In 1933, George obtained permission from the Meteorological Office to set up his own weather station.

George, aged eight.

DID YOU KNOW ?

Finding only occasional and temporary local teaching posts, George was permanently broke and depended on a borrowed telescope for his observations. During this time George's drawings of comets and the planets impressed several eminent BAA members. In 1937, he secured a full-time teaching post and meteor watching then had to be fitted into a strict routine of daily life. He recalled in later years: 'If it promised to be clear, I'd leave school at 4.30pm, go home for tea and then go to bed until 8pm, observe from 8.15pm till 1am, or 3am if there was a lot of activity.'

From 1939 to 1945 George experienced some alarming wartime escapades, including three court martials with the RAF in North Africa and Italy for observing the sky at night when he should have been on night duty. After the Second World War he returned to teaching in Peterborough – first at Southfields Junior School and then Fletton Secondary School – and, of course, he continued with his absolute fascination of astronomy. He was utterly absorbed in the scientific study of the universe, especially of the motions, positions, sizes, composition, and behaviour of objects in the sky. He once confessed to us that the best part was studying the data and interpreting it as far as the science of the stars, planets and other objects are concerned. He didn't have any fancy equipment to study the sky – so sketching or painting his observations enabled him to recall events more than any photograph could or would be able to do.

In 1953, George embarked on a five-year search for a comet. He was not optimistic as none had been discovered in England since 1894. However, that was all to change. On 25 August 1959 he discovered his first comet and five days later became instantly famous by finding another! Celebrity, however, was not for him, as he was a shy and modest man who tried hard to avoid the attentions of the media. Comets Alcock three and four were discovered in March 1963 and September 1965, respectively. Again, on 8 July 1967, George broke another record as no new novae had been discovered by anyone anywhere since 1964 until George spotted one. The very next day the Royal Observatory confirmed his find: 'Nova Delphini, the first nova discovered from England since 1934.'

Success continued as some nine months later George found his second nova and for a brief period the two novae discovered were simultaneously visible to the naked eye. The

George star gazing, 1967.

last of his discoveries included Nova Herculis in 1991 (the fastest nova ever recorded!), which brought him the record for discoveries of comets and novae.

Astronomy, however, was only one of George's many passions. He told us that he spent more hours studying birds, botany and church architecture, than the skies. That said, he had no doubt that his greatest achievement was the years he spent teaching.

He received an MBE 'for services to astronomy' in 1979 and a minor planet (3174) was named in his honour. George died on 15 December 2000.

DID YOU KNOW ?

In April 2005 a plaque commemorating George's lifetime achievements in astronomy was unveiled at Peterborough Cathedral.

36. The Fab Four in Peterborough

The Beatles played at the Embassy Theatre (now a branch of Edwards pubs) on 2 December 1962 supporting crooner Frank Ifield. Their manager Brian Epstein had successfully arranged for them to perform alongside Ifield. Sadly, critics reported that they were a flop with fans, who had come to see their idol Frank Ifield, saying that they were truly dreadful. Promoter Arthur Howes was quoted as saying that the audience 'sat on their hands during the mop tops' performance'.

However, the Beatles were not to be daunted for long and returned to the city on 17 March 1963 as part of their tour with Tommy Roe and Chris Montez. Thankfully, their reception was far better than on their troubled show with Frank Ifield months earlier, and their setlist of six songs included 'Love Me Do', 'Do You Want To Know A Secret', 'A Taste of Honey', 'I Saw Her Standing There' and 'Please Please Me', which went down a storm.

Embassy Theatre, Broadway.

DID YOU KNOW ?

Paul McCartney said that the best thing that came out of their first gig at Peterborough was that they met Ted Taylor, lead singer of the Ted Taylor Four, who taught them how to use stage makeup.

Paul McCartney is quoted as saying:

> Ted Taylor first told us how to use make-up. We were playing the Embassy Cinema at Peterborough late that year, very low on the bill to Frank Ifield and below The Ted Taylor Four as well. Ted had a funny little synth on the end of his piano on which he could play tunes like Sooty. He would use it for Telstar - the audience went wild to hear his synth sound. It was Ted that said, 'You looked a little pale out there, lads. You should use make-up.' We asked him how. He said, 'There's this pancake stuff, Leichner 27. You can get it from the chemist. Take a little pad and rub it on; it gives you a tan. And put a black line around your eyes and lips.' We said, 'That's a bit dodgy, isn't it?' He said, 'Believe me, they will never see it, and you'll look good.'
>
> Right afterwards we were being photographed for a poster for Blackpool. They had been bootlegging posters, which meant we were obviously getting quite popular, and the poster company said we should do an official one. So, they did four squares - one of us in each square. And you can see the black line around our eyes. We never lived it down!

In October 1962 they recorded 'Love Me Do' at EMI studios (later known as Abbey Road) in London with producer George Martin. At this time, they were famous in Liverpool and had to wear disguises to go out during the day. It wasn't until the release of their second single, 'Please Please Me', in January 1963 that they became nationally famous.

Beatles ephemera.

Their single 'Love Me Do' was 17th in the pop chart when they started their extensive touring (nationally and internationally) from 1963 to 1966. It was during this period that the world woke up to the Fab Four and when Beatlemania was born along with a worldwide love of British rock music, clothes, culture and heritage. Thus, Britain's decade of the swinging '60s really took off and the world went mad for all things British. By early 1964 the Beatles became international stars and led the so-called British invasion of the United States pop market.

37. The Smallpox Lady

Lady Mary Montagu (née Pierrepont) was a diarist for fifty years (1712–62), allowing today's generation into the affairs of heart, travel and politics nearly 300 years ago.

She married Edward Wortley Montagu in 1712 and is deemed one of the most important women writers between Aphra Behn (judged the first English professional female literary dramatist/writer from the late seventeenth century) and Jane Austen. Lady Montagu is viewed as one of the most provocative and entertaining writers of her time.

DID YOU KNOW ?
Montagu's husband, Sir Edward Wortley Montagu, was known generally as 'Mr Wortley' and was twice MP for Peterborough (1734–47 and 1754–61).

Etching of Lady Mary Wortley Montagu.

Mary's husband was appointed Ambassador to Turkey on 7 April 1716, taking Mary with him to Turkey where she discovered the practice of inoculation against smallpox. Lady Mary returned to England with knowledge of the Ottoman practice of inoculation against smallpox, known as variolation. In Asia, practitioners developed the variolation technique of deliberate infection with smallpox. Dried smallpox scabs were blown into the nose of an individual who then contracted a mild form of the disease. Upon recovery the individual was immune to smallpox. Of those variolated 1–2 per cent died, as compared to 30 per cent who died when they contracted the disease naturally. In the 1790s, Edward Jenner developed a safer method, using vaccination.

DID YOU KNOW ?

A sun obelisk, erected in 1747 by William Wentworth, the 3rd Earl Fitzwilliam (of Milton Hall) can be found at the former Fitzwilliam country seat of Wentworth Woodhouse near Rotherham. It acknowledges Lady Mary's 'intellectual achievements' and it is said to be the only Georgian monument to a woman erected in her lifetime.

Lady Mary had various lovers throughout her life, including the poet Alexander Pope who suffered from Pott's disease (tuberculosis of the bone) and had stopped growing at 4 feet 6 inches, becoming humpbacked with impaired sight, and in almost constant pain with headaches and respiratory troubles. The years 1715–16 were his healthiest and this is when his love affair with Lady Mary fully blossomed. Lady Mary's affair with Pope cooled over time and by 1727 their relationship had turned to complete mutual enmity.

Obelisk at Wentworth Woodhouse.

In July 1739 Lady Mary became estranged from her husband and again left England for Europe and Asia. Her husband spent his last years hoarding money. At his death on 22 January 1761, aged eighty-two, he was said to have been a millionaire.

As Whig MP for Peterborough, Edward Wortley Montagu purchased and transferred two houses on the south side of Westgate fronting Boroughbury (town end of Lincoln Road) and 4 acres of grassland between Westgate and Cowgate 'for the better accommodation of the poor of the Peterborough Parish of St John the Baptist'. Wortley's workhouse, later known as the Westgate Almshouses, was rebuilt in 1774 to provide mixed accommodation for those destitute, orphaned, old or imbecile. In 1837, it was largely rebuilt again to house more of the poor and vagrant in the parish.

Upon Edward's death, Mary's daughter the Countess of Bute, begged her mother to return to England. Eventually Lady Mary came home a year after her husband's death at the time when her son-in-law John Stuart, 3rd Earl of Bute was prime minister (1762–63). Society at this time viewed marriage as sacrosanct. The media refrained to treat sexual infringement with open salacious enjoyment as it used to, but now treated any infringements with outright condemnation. An intriguing turnaround considering that Lady Mary's son-in-law had been involved with the Princess of Wales – perhaps that worked its way into Lady Mary's diaries.

DID YOU KNOW ?

For half a century Lady Mary kept a diary with sharp-eyed observations and satirical comments. These volumes were left to her daughter, the Countess Bute, who for obvious reasons had most of them burnt after her mother's death on 21 August 1762 at No. 28 Berkeley Square, London, aged seventy-three.

38. Secret Agent Tiny Mitchell

At the bridge south of the River Nene was Bridge House, the offices of Mitchell Engineering Ltd, who also had works at Glebe Road and Fengate. The company was founded in London in 1933 by Frederick 'Fred' G. Mitchell (1885–1962) as the Mitchell Conveyor and Transporter Co. Fred, a completely self-made man, was nicknamed 'Tiny' as he was 6 feet 4.5 inches tall with a bulk to match. He was born in London and at the age of fourteen he became an apprentice on the railway, serving his time in the engineering office at Nine Elms. He then graduated to the railway drawing office. After that he found work as a draughtsman with a firm of consulting engineers, where he gained experience of various engineering jobs, including the Ritz Hotel, the Gaiety Theatre, and the designing of bridges (some in India).

His next career move was to the engineering firm Fraser & Chalmers, where he became head of the machine-planning department, working on the design of machines to deal with any contingency in clearing and construction work. The latter created a civilian job for him during the First World War. He was attached to the French Army to try to stem the retreat to the Marne with his trench-digging machinery. Then he was transferred to Kitchener's staff in Paris where he became a 'trouble shooter' for Kitchener.

When the First World War was over, at the age of thirty-three he took the rash step of setting up on his own. He started without a penny and won a contract to build a coal handling plant at a Birmingham power station making him £40,000. The success of this project led to other power station contracts.

DID YOU KNOW ?

In 1940, Mitchell's moved from its premises in London to Peterborough because of the destruction created by the Blitz.

Some fourteen years later David Mitchell took over management of the business and success led to more success. In 1962, Mitchell's acquired Kinnear Moodie, a leading tunneling business. The range of products included boilers, mechanical handling plant, overhead transmission lines, ropeways, food preparation machinery, mechanical car parks and galvanizing.

Mitchell was the chief company of a group whose activities included the design of atomic power plants to the manufacture of pea-shelling machines. Mitchell exported its

Bridge House mural.

Tiny with one of his boats at Cowes, IOW.

mechanical handling equipment and boilers – found in many power stations in many parts of the world – plus other big engineering projects such as harbours, ore plants and power schemes.

The company extended its interest in nuclear power when it concluded an agreement with A. M. F. Atomics Incorporation of New York to design and construct atomoic power plants in most parts of the world.

Another important side of Mitchell's activities was civil construction work carried out by Mitchell Construction Co. Ltd with its headquarters at Bridge House (architect Howard V. Loss & Partners), Peterborough. It constructed the atomic power station at Chapel Cross, near Annan, in Dumfriesshire and erected dams for the north of Scotland hydro-electric scheme.

Mitchell Ropeways Ltd was another associate company headquartered at Peterborough.

Two years before Tiny's death he financed Rotocraft, a business that developed the grasshopper helicopter in partnership with its designer J. S. Shapiro.

Sadly, in 1973, Mitchell Construction Ltd (Peterborough) became defunct under its managing director, David Morrell. The company employed 5,000 staff, turning over £500 million in today's terms and at one time simultaneously holding the world records for hard and soft rock tunneling.

DID YOU KNOW ?

The site of the former Bridge House is under construction as part of the Fletton Quays developments and the former Mitchell building's interesting murals depicting the city's industrial history is to be reinstated as part of the entrance to the Quays from Town Bridge.

The site of the former Bridge House today.

39. Torpedo City

In 1889 John Percy Hall left Jarrow to take up the position of managing director of John Penn & Sons Ltd, Greenwich (closed in 1914). While working there he had the control of the design and building of war vessel ranging from battleships to destroyers and scouts.

During 1899 John Percy Hall (b.1846 and married to Georgina Clavering) founded his company J. P. Hall & Sons Engineers in Peterborough with production starting a year later in 1900. The factory was situated off London Road in Queens Walk and initially manufactured direct-acting pumps, designed by John Hall, himself.

From very small beginnings the company made a name for itself in the manufacture of marine and electric lighting station pumps for boiler feeding, vertical direct acting cargo oil pumps, transfer and pipe line pumps, air and service pumps for various purposes.

During the First World War they were under government control on submarine work, tank parts, and battleship accessories. Sadly, on 18 January 1917, John Percy Hall died at his home 'Carville', Lawrie Park Road, Sydenham at the age of seventy. He was a member of the Institute of Mechanical Engineers and he was one of the first members of the North-East Coast Institution of Engineers and Shipbuilders (formed in 1884).

His sons John P. Hall Jr and Gilbert C. Hall took over the business during the First World War. After this the company had around 200 employees and capital of £30,000.

The workforce was said to be fiercely patriotic after the sinking of the Lusitania in 1915 when it was torpedoed and sunk by a German U-boat, causing the deaths of nearly 2,000 passengers and crew. Thus, it is perhaps not surprising that management and employees

Right: John Percy Hall *c.* 1882.

Below: Raising money for the war effort.

took to heart the severe loss of lives on the ocean liner, given that the firm was contracted by the Admiralty to manufacture submarine pumps and battleship accessories to win the war at sea.

After the Second World War J. P. Hall & Sons specialised in equipment for oil tankers and oil refineries and its machinery was exported all over the world.

Regal Place.

Sadly, the cessation of over sixty years of manufacture of industrial and marine pumps in this city ended abruptly in 1963. Today the site of the factory is occupied by blocks of flats.

40. The Fitzwilliams and the Kennedys

The Milton estate consisted of 23,300 acres extending along the Nene Valley roughly between Peterborough and Irthlingborough. The founder was merchant taylor Sir William Fitzwilliam, a merchant of the Staple of Calais and an Alderman of the City of London, who was knighted in around 1515. The oldest part of Milton Hall is the north front, which was probably built in the period around 1590–1610. It was not until the mid-eighteenth century that the 3rd Earl was able to enlarge the hall by commissioning the architect Henry Flitcroft to design the imposing south front in the Palladian style.

The Fitzwilliams also owned Wentworth Woodhouse, near Rotherham, South Yorkshire – a 365-room house that is twice the size of Buckingham Palace. They had it built in the early eighteenth century and owned it up until 1989, when it was bought by Clifford Newbold and his sons Paul, Marcus and Giles. In addition to Wentworth estate, which was financed largely by the Fitzwilliam's ownership of coalfields – dubbed 'black diamonds' in

Yorkshire – they also owned most of the land in the Irish counties of Wicklow and Tyrone, and more recently Bourne Park estate, near Canterbury.

DID YOU KNOW ?
The Fitzwilliams can trace their ancestry back to William the Conqueror and today's Tory MP and prominent Catholic, the Right Honorable Jacob Rees-Mogg (MP for North East Somerset) is married to Helena de Chair, daughter of Lady Tadgell (only child of the 8th Earl Fitzwilliam).

As a family, the Fitzwilliams were the subject of numerous scandals and it's said that letters and other paperwork were placed on a huge bonfire at Wentworth and involved three weeks of continuous burning!

The 7th Earl was accused of being swapped with an unwanted Fitzwilliam girl at birth. William 'Billy' Fitzwilliam had to defend his rights to the estate in court. Furthermore his son Peter, 8th Earl Fitzwilliam, did nothing to respect his father's struggle to keep the properties and land in the family. In fact, the 8th Earl Fitzwilliam spent most of his time on the French Riviera womanising with his best friend Aly Khan, the son of the Aga Khan.

Kathleen with her brother JFK.

Peter married Olive 'Obby' Plunket (daughter of the Archbishop of Dublin) in 1933 but due to her dependence on alcohol the marriage soon started to flounder and Peter (a Protestant) found himself drawn to the glamorous and enchanting Kathleen 'Kick' Kennedy – younger sister of the future 35th President of the United States, John F. Kennedy. Kathleen was at this time the Dowager Duchess of Devonshire. Kick's parents Joe and Rose Kennedy, being staunch Catholics, found it hard to accept Peter, 8th Earl Fitzwilliam. Joe Kennedy, once US Ambassador to the UK (1938–40), while not overly keen on the marriage of his daughter to a Protestant, was far more understanding than his wife Rose.

Kick knew that if Peter were to divorce Obby then it would mean an irreparable break with her family. It seems she was prepared to elope with Peter but tragically she and Peter died in a plane crash during a violent storm in the Cevennes Mountains in France. The Dove plane piloted by Townhend and co-pilot Freeman was on its way from Cannes to Paris on 13 May 1948 with only Peter and Kick as passengers. They were scheduled to meet Kick's father at the George V Hotel in Paris to discuss marriage plans.

Wreckage of the plane crash.

The plane was found nose down with both pilot and co-pilot crumpled against the cockpit with hankies in their mouths – a standard procedure in a crash landing to avoid biting the tongue. Peter was found crushed beneath his seat while Kick was found fastened by her seat belt in a skewed position with her legs broken. An enquiry later stated that they would have known of their impending deaths for around ten seconds.

Thus, the only male person to inherit Milton Hall, Wentworth and other lands and estates was Peter's cousin Eric Wentworth Fitzwilliam, who became 9th Earl.

When the 9th Earl died in 1952 without issue, the title came back again to the branch of the family at Milton. Four years later the tenth (and last) Earl, Tom Fitzwilliam married Lady FitzAlan-Howard, but they had no children either. Following the earl's death in 1979, the Milton estates descended through the Countess's family from her first marriage, initially to her daughter Lady Elizabeth Anne Hastings and then to her grandson, Sir Phillip Naylor-Leyland.

Kathleen's grave at Edensor, Derbyshire.

Philip Vivyan Naylor-Leyland (b. 9 Aug 1953) succeeded his father as baronet in 1987. He married Lady Isabella Lambton in 1980 and they and their family are the current occupants. Milton Hall remains the largest private house near Peterborough.

DID YOU KNOW ?
During the Falklands War, on Friday 30 April 1982, Margaret Thatcher and her husband Denis stayed overnight at Milton.

If the walls and grounds of Milton Hall could speak they would tell a fine story of Britain's aristocracy, socialites, politicians, and wartime secrets.

41. X-Ray Man

Alfred Caleb Taylor was born in Newark, Nottinghamshire, on 29 December 1860. In 1880, he started work as a dispenser at Peterborough Infirmary (now the museum) in Priestgate, succeeding Mr Whitwell. Dr Paley was then physician and Mr Thomas Walker was surgeon.

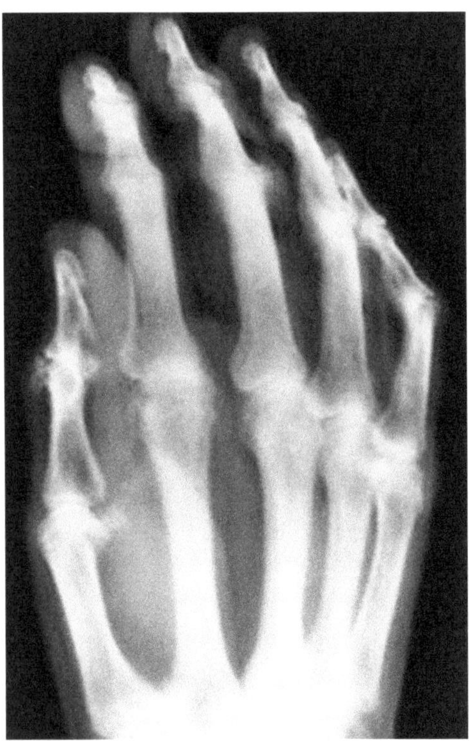

Hand X-ray, *c.* 1898.

Caleb, as he preferred to be known, was an early promoter of X-ray technology and he designed and built his own equipment at the infirmary in 1896. His machine was the first outside London and was powered by batteries (accumulators), which were recharged at Cadge & Coleman, the local flour mill as there was no public electricity supply at this time. His device ranked as the first in the UK outside London and took positive rather than negative images. Back then the dangers of prolonged exposure to radiation were unknown. Caleb's work was pioneering in the medical world, but it exacted an enormous price as he used himself in his X-ray experiments. Ultimately this caused him to have three fingers on his left hand and one on his right hand amputated. Eventually, Caleb contracted radiation poisoning, but he expressed no regrets. This pioneering X-ray work finally cost him his life and he died of skin cancer on 26 July 1927.

Caleb had a keen interest in photography, which was shared with his relatives Andrew and George Taylor (A&G Taylor, photographers to Queen Victoria under a royal warrant dated 1886). They claimed to be the largest photographers in the world, with national and international offices. In fact, Caleb Taylor was a founder member of the Peterborough Photographic Society in 1916 and was its president from then until his death.

DID YOU KNOW ?

Caleb's other interests included art and music (he was a member of the local Operatic and Orchestral societies). In addition, he was on the committee of Peterborough Archaeological Society and a member of the Natural History Society.

He served as radiographer and secretary (a managerial position) at the infirmary from 1889 until he retired in September 1926, when he was presented with a £700 cheque and a silver salver in recognition of his sacrifice to the advancement of pioneering X-ray machines that served to assist with early diagnosis of medical conditions.

However, these early X-ray machines were highly rudimentary in the way they were pieced together, as well as the fact that they discharged shockingly high levels of radiation – both to the operator and the patient.

DID YOU KNOW ?

An 1896 X-ray machine exposed the body to 1,500 times more radiation than modern technology does. This is mainly because each image took ninety minutes to develop, which in turn dramatically increased the patient's cumulative exposure to the rays. In comparison, modern X-rays require 21 milliseconds and technicians place lead covering over the body to protect vital organs from the slightest exposure.

X-ray machine, *c.* 1910.

Pioneering experimenters like Caleb used these early X-ray machines, which often caused them to suffer effects such as eye complaints, skin burns, loss of hair, cancers and premature death. Caleb's X-ray tube was acquired by South Kensington Museum to form part of their exhibits on the development of X-ray research.

On his death Caleb left a widow, four sons and three daughters. His funeral took place at the Peterborough Cathedral at 2 p.m. on 29 July 1927 followed by interment at St Botolph's Church, Longthorpe.

Acknowledgements

In compiling the content for this book, we sought to ensure that the text is factually correct to the best of our knowledge, enthralling and stimulating. The authors are indebted to the following people, we could not have done it without them: the late Messrs Harry Miles; John Jack Gaunt; Harry Hurst; John Seeley; George Dixon; Stanley Hoare; George Alcock; the late Miss Norah Hartley; the late Mr and Mrs John; Josephine Gillatt, and the late Mr and Mrs Harry and Gwen Hurst. Special thanks go to Jean Miles, Doreen Foster, Heidi Semple, Vera Seeley, Kathleen Church, and John and Grace Foster.

Bibliography

Alcock, G. E. D., *A Glimpse at English Architecture: Churches.*

Alcock, G. E. D., *A Glimpse at English Architecture: Houses, Castles etc.*

Arrowsmith, A. Louis, *Longthorpe and its Environs – A Microcosm of a Village* (1984).

Bricks Without Straw (Old Fletton: Hicks & Co. Ltd, 1924).

Bull, June and Vernon, *A History of Peterborough Parish Church (1407–2007)* (Express Printing, 2007).

Bull, June and Vernon, *Peterborough: A Portrait in Old Picture Postcards* (S. B. Publications, 1988).

Bull, June and Vernon, *Peterborough History Tour* (Amberley Publishing, 2014).

Bull, June and Vernon, *Peterborough Now and Then in Colour* (The History Press, 2013).

Bull, June and Vernon, *Peterborough Through Time* (Amberley Publishing, 2009).

Bull, June and Vernon, *Peterborough Through Time: A Second Selection* (Amberley Publishing, 2011).

Bull, June and Vernon, McKenzie, Rita, *Peterborough: Then and Now: A Portrait in Photographs and Old Postcards* (S. B. Publications, 1992).

Bull, J. and V., Perry, S., and Sturgess, R., *Peterborough: A Third Portrait in Old Picture Postcards* (S. B. Publications, 1990).

'Century Story 1854–1954', *Peterborough Advertiser.*

Directories of Peterborough and District: 1838, 1848, 1870, 1898, 1901, 1907,1922, 1925, 1927, 1940, 1952, 1959, 1961, 1963, 1969, 1973.

Hornsey, Brian, *Ninety Years of Cinema in Peterborough* (1998).

Hillier, Richard, *Clay That Burns: A History of The Fletton Brick Industry* (1981).

Mellows, William Thomas, 'Orton Waterville', reprinted from the annual report of the Peterborough Natural History, Scientific and Archaeological Society (1922).

Millet, Terry, *Some History and Tales of Orton Longueville* (1993).

Peterborough Citizen

Northampton Sites and Monuments Record.

Perry, Stephen, *Peterborough: A Portrait in Old Picture Postcards: Vol. 2* (S. B. Publications, 1989).

Peterborough, Borough Guide No. 218 (Edward J. Burrow, 1904).

Pevsner, N., *The Buildings of England: Northamptonshire* (1961).

Sweeting, Revd W. D., *Historical and Architectural Notes on the Parish Churches in and Around Peterborough* (1868).

Victoria County History IV.